Companion Prayer Book
to the
Liturgy of the Hours

Companion Prayer Book

to the
Liturgy of the Hours

Georges-Albert Boissinot

Catholic Book Publishing Corp.
New Jersey

NIHIL OBSTAT: Rev. Msgr. James M. Cafone, M.A., S.T.D.
Censor Librorum

IMPRIMATUR: ✠ Most Rev. John J. Myers, J.C.D., D.D.
Archbishop of Newark

(T-434)

ISBN 978-0-89942-354-8

© 2010 Catholic Book Publishing Corp., New Jersey

Printed in the USA

www.catholicbookpublishing.com

CONTENTS

FOREWORD

The reform of the liturgy that came out of Vatican II replaced the old *Breviary* with a wonderful book, in tune with our times: *The Liturgy of the Hours*.[1] This renewal of the liturgy which concerns not only priests, but also members of religious communities and lay people, was inspired by the great tradition of the past, but also meets the needs of this day and age. It is without a doubt one of the most valuable contributions of Vatican II. However, in order for it to achieve all its goals, this profound reform requires a new way of thinking and an effective theological, liturgical and spiritual education. As a matter of fact, Vatican II expressly states that priests and all those who participate in the Divine Office should have a better knowledge of the liturgy and the Bible, especially of the psalms (SC 90).[2]

Using the *General Instruction* (GI) *of the Liturgy of the Hours* as a starting point, these pages aim at helping the reader to participate more fully in the prayer of the Church. This way, the celebration of the Hours will nourish one's

---

[1] *The Liturgy of the Hours*, Totowa, NJ: Catholic Book Publishing Corp., 1975/1976. It is highly recommended to read the Apostolic Constitution *Laudis Canticum* by Paul VI who promulgated the Divine Office as revised by a decree from the Vatican II Council; and also, the *General Instruction of the Liturgy of the Hours*.

[2] To refer to the Council's Constitution on the liturgy, we shall use SC for *Sacrosanctum Concilium*, and GI for *General Instruction of the Liturgy of the Hours*.

faith and "the soul will be more in tune with the voice."

Georges-Albert Boissinot, r.s.v.

1

THE LITURGY OF THE HOURS

There are so many ways . . .

There are so many ways to praise the Lord.

There are so many ways to celebrate the *Liturgy of the Hours*.

As soon as I arrived at the seminary, I was expected to attend Sunday Vespers. When I think about it today, I am amazed that we were given a big Roman and Gregorian Prayer Book and that we had to sing the psalms without having a word of explanation about them. On Sunday evenings, before bedtime, we used to celebrate Compline, with the unforgettable *In manus tuas, Domine* (Into your hands, O Lord, I commit my spirit). Things were different then. I still remember my joy when I started to understand the Latin words of the *Magnificat*. Later, at the theological seminary, I became interested in studying the psalms. When WWII was over, we started receiving the religious journal *Maison-Dieu* and other publications that opened up for me new vistas on the Divine Office. What a discovery that was! To this day, I miss the beauty of the Marian antiphons and of some Gregorian responses, among others, the hymns for Christmas and Holy Week. Not everything was bad before Vatican II!

In 1962, I left for Brazil.[3] On November 1, I spent the day in Rio de Janeiro, at the historic Sâo Bento (Saint Benedict) Monastery, which stood at the end of Dom Gerardo Street, facing the Bay of Guanabara and the Island of Cobras, far from the hustle and bustle of the big city.

Vatican II was just beginning and the liturgy had not yet been reformed. At dawn and in the evening, the Benedictine monks would sing Lauds and Vespers, in beautiful Gregorian chant, before the statue of Our Lady of Montserrat that towered above the magnificent baroque altarpiece. It was All Saints Day, and there reigned in the church an atmosphere of silent reverence. The beauty of the sculptures and the chanting inspired the faithful to unite with all the Saints in heaven to glorify the Lord.

Many years later, I had the chance of going to Paris. On the solemn occasion of Pentecost, I went to Notre Dame cathedral; the nave and the sides were full, as on every Friday afternoon. Vespers began with Psalm 141. As the swirls of incense slowly drifted through the air, the congregation started singing: "Let my prayer rise like incense."

The hymn to the Holy Spirit, the psalms, the reading of the Word of God, the singing of the *Magnificat* all constitute a liturgy both simple and solemn which appeals to many people and gives rise to fervent prayer in the midst of a mod-

---

[3] The author lived in Brazil for 18 years and in Rome for 9.

ern metropolis. The celebration ended with the singing of an antiphon to Our Lady and Exposition of the Blessed Sacrament, according to medieval tradition. When the service was over, two Protestant ladies from the Netherlands said to me: "We didn't know that Catholics could pray so well. This reconciles us with the Catholic Church."

Prayer is a wonderful feast. (Max Thurian)

In Assisi, the enchanting city of Francis and Clare, a vigil was being held for Saint Rufinus, martyr and first bishop of Assisi. On the evening of August 10, the bishop, a great devotee of the liturgy, was presiding over the Office of the Readings. The congregation sang the psalms. After the proclamation of the Word and the reading of the life of the church's founder, the bishop delivered the homily. Then, all the faithful went down to the crypt and gathered around the tomb of Saint Rufinus, there to profess their faith by reciting the Apostles' Creed. It was a significant and moving gesture.

Still in Assisi, at the Monastery of the Poor Clares in a quiet chapel, the Hours are sung in French to the sounds of sacred and tasteful music. In the chapel are gathered pilgrims and tourists, young and old, members of religious orders and lay people. Here is another place that reveals a sense of deep contemplation and a rich liturgy, in the footsteps of Francis, the *Poverello*, and Clare.

Going to Brazil, to a modest parish church in the state of Sâo Paolo, a few monks chant the evening service, joined by a group of illiterate persons who, naturally, cannot follow the psalms in a book. And yet, these good people repeat the antiphons, sing *Glory to the Father*, listen carefully to the readings, recite their prayers out loud, and raise their hands to pray the *Our Father*. Such is the liturgical prayer of the most humble of people. With a little imagination, it is quite possible to make the Church's prayer accessible to all the Christian faithful.

There are so many ways to celebrate the Hours. But one must believe in this prayer, and each community must find its own way to praise the Lord.

It doesn't matter whether one stands to sing a hymn or the Gospel, or sits to listen to the reading from the Scriptures; whether one bows as a sign of worship or respect, or makes the Sign of the Cross on oneself. (Joseph Gelineau)

2

PRAYER IN THE OLD TESTAMENT

Christian prayer has developed from the practices of Israel. Our ancestors in the faith have given us the 150 psalms. *Tehillim* in Hebrew, which means praise, the psalms were sung to the accompaniment of a string instrument, the psaltery, hence their name, but also of "the pleasant harp and the lyre" (Ps 81:3). They expressed the joys, the anguish, the fears, the suffering, the hopes, and the trust, not only of their authors, but of an entire people. Throughout the centuries, they have been altered, renewed, adapted, polished like the stones of our old churches. The psalms were used both as personal and communal prayer.

The Sacred Books also contain many Canticles, in particular from Isaiah and Sirach, and the Book of Wisdom.

Psalms were sung during the great liturgical celebrations in the Temple, such as processions and pilgrimages. The renowned monument had been built at great expense by King Solomon in the 10th century B.C., and had been destroyed by Nebuchadnezzar's armies in 587 B.C. After the people's exile, the second Temple was erected on the same spot, and it was restored by Herod the Great. It would take almost eighty years to finish the restoration, from the year 20 B.C. to A.D. 65, that is five years before the final destruction of the Temple. The people took great pride in it: on top of the hill of Zion, it glittered from all its gold. Three times a year—for Passover, the Festival of Lights *(Hanukkah)* and the Feast of Tabernacles *(Sukkot)*, Israelites would go to the Temple proclaiming the psalms of ascent. As they arrived, the joyful pilgrims would sing:

> And finally our feet are standing
> at your gates, O Jerusalem.
> Jerusalem is built as a city
> that is firmly bound together in unity.
>
> (Ps 122:2-3)

For the people of the Lord, the Temple was the heart of its religion, and central to all solemn processions and great feasts, as well as to the daily worship.

> Holding leafy branches, join in the festal procession
> up to the horns of the altar   (Ps 118:27)

In the sanctuary of the Temple, the priests offered sacrifices in the morning and in the evening; the animal offerings were charred and grilled over a fire and the smoke of the sacrifice rose toward the Lord. Incense was also thrown into the fire and it would drift up in scented curls.

> May my prayer be like incense before You,
> the lifting up of my hands like the evening
> sacrifice.   (Ps 141:2)

Saint Luke tells us that Zechariah "was designated by lot to enter the sanctuary of the Lord and offer incense" (1:9).

In the synagogue, the weekly worship consisted of the reading from the Torah, the Law, and from the other Scriptures, the singing of psalms, and the rabbi's commentaries. It is the form which shaped our Liturgy of the Word.

Families also had their own liturgy: besides reciting the *Shema Israel* and the *Eighteen Benedictions*, they prayed three times a day, at nine in the morning, noon, and in the middle of the afternoon, that is, at terce, sext and none.[4] There was the great annual celebration of Passover, with its paschal meal *(seder)* of lamb, unleavened bread and bitter herbs, which followed a very precise ritual.

The first disciples of the risen Christ did not abruptly sever their ties to the Temple. Acts 2:46 tells us that "they would assemble together in the Temple." Peter and John can be seen going up to the Temple "for the hour of prayer at three o'clock in the afternoon" (3:1).

Israel gave us the psalms and the books of the First Covenant. Our Easter and Pentecost have their distant origins in their equivalent Jewish feasts.[5]

---

[4] According to the old Roman calendar, the day was divided into four three-hour periods and the night into four vigils (prime, terce, sext and none).

[5] See Acts 5:20-21, 42.

3

JESUS' PRAYER

Since liturgy is a way of worshiping God through Christ and His Mystical Body, we cannot understand it without contemplating Jesus' own prayer.

By becoming incarnate, the Son of God brings to this world the eternal praise He gives His Father within the Trinity. Jesus comes to glorify God through His entire life and His continuous prayer. During His existence on earth, He prays as the beloved Son, as Head of the new humanity and Supreme Priest of the New Covenant.

The most beautiful of the sons of men offers to the Lord an ineffable poem of love and praise. Sublime words overflow from His heart, and His tongue is like the pen of a skillful scribe, says Psalm 45:2.

As a small child, Jesus learned His first prayers with Mary and Joseph; mornings and evenings, the family from Nazareth recited the *Shema Israel: Hark, Israel, the Lord your God is the Only One. . . .* They gave thanks to the Lord before all of their activities and before all meals. Like all the boys of His age, Mary's Son attended His village's synagogue school. He learned to read the Scriptures in Hebrew and recite the 150 psalms. Every year, just like His contemporaries,

Jesus joined the pilgrimages to Jerusalem to go and pray in the Temple, whose splendor He greatly admired. For Him, the Temple was His Father's house; there, He truly was "in His Father's house," as He states when He is twelve (Lk 2:49).

In the Gospels, we see Jesus praying during the night and very early in the morning, alone, on the mountain, and in the desert. Luke emphasizes this aspect of the Lord's ritual: "It was in those days that He went onto the mountain to pray, and He spent the entire night in prayer to God" (Lk 6:12). Mark also says: "Early the next morning, long before dawn, He arose and went off to a secluded place, where He prayed" (Mk 1:35).

Our Savior starts praying in the most solemn moments: at the time of His baptism and of His transfiguration, before multiplying the loaves of bread, before Lazarus' resurrection, before choosing His Apostles, after His miracles. Jesus blesses the "Lord of heaven and earth . . ." (Lk 10:21).

Jesus also takes part in the liturgy of His people when He goes to the synagogue on the Sabbath, "as is the custom" or when He makes a pilgrimage to the Holy City. During the paschal meal—the seder—He recites the psalms and the hymns of the Blessing, thereby being faithful to the Jewish tradition. St. John mentions the magnificent prayer that follows the Last Supper, in which the Master glorifies the Father and beseeches Him on behalf of His disciples and for all His followers until the end of time.

Before His passion, prostrated in agony, Jesus prays for a long time, repeating in His mother tongue: *"Abba"* (Mk 14:36), a loving word which means "daddy," "dearly beloved father." On the Cross, He begs forgiveness for His executioners: "Father, forgive them, for they do not know what they are doing" (Lk 23:34). In desperation He prays Psalm 22: "My God, My God, why have You forsaken Me?" (Mk 15:34-35).

"The Word," writes Pius XII, "proclaims and extols in the Psalms the absolute greatness of God" *(Mediator Dei)*. He has given the psalms their full meaning. In just a few words, Saint Augustine says it well: "Christ is the great cantor of the psalms" *(iste cantator psalmorum)*.

> The psalms never sounded as true as in the mouth and the heart of Jesus.
>
> (Michel Hubaut)

In the Letter to the Hebrews, we read: "During the course of His earthly life, Jesus offered up prayer and petitions with loud cries to the One Who had the power to save Him from death, and He was heard because of His godly fear"(Heb 5:7).

Redeemer and Priest, King of the universe, Jesus praises, worships, gives thanks, and implores in the name and on behalf of sinful humanity. His whole life is one of worship and praise that rise to heaven as a great symphony of love and thanksgiving. Jesus lives in communion with the Father and His prayer is the very "soul of His messianic ministry" (GI 4). Jesus prays through the action of the Holy Spirit (Lk 10:21).

In His eternal glory, the risen Christ doesn't stop giving praise and, forever living, He continues to intercede for humanity. Leader of the Angels and of the Saints, Shepherd and victorious Lamb, He strikes up the hymn of the heavenly liturgy before the throne of the thrice Holy, as John describes Him in the Book of Revelation.

Therefore, Jesus carries out His priestly mission within the Church by the celebration of the Eucharist, but also "by other means, in particular in the Divine Office, through his unceasing praise of the Father and interceding for the salvation of the world" (SC 83).

It is a prayer without end in time. When I say it, others are asleep and when I sleep, others are saying it.

4

THE PRAYER OF THE CHURCH

Together with Christ, seated at the right hand of the Father, we who are pilgrims on earth already participate in the heavenly liturgy. Our prayer prolongs until the end of time the praise given first by God's only Son when He was in this world.

The Master Himself urged His followers to pray all the time: "Then Jesus told them a parable about the need for them to pray always and never to lose heart" (Lk 18:1). In His ecclesiastical sermon (Mt 18:20), He reminds His disciples of the value of communal prayer: "For where two or three are gathered together in My Name, I am there in their midst." Joining in prayer gives us unlimited strength in obtaining all we ask for. "If you ask the Father for anything in My Name, He will give it to you" (Jn 16:23). Above all, Jesus bestows the Holy Spirit upon us and teaches us how to pray and live like sons and daughters of God, following the example of the divine Son in prayer. The prayer of the Church thus perpetuates the Lord's own prayer; said in union with Him and inspired by His Spirit, it leads us to the Father. Saint Cyprian emphasized the power of prayer from Christians united with their bishop.

From the very beginning, the disciples understood this mystery. Luke describes the attitude of the early community: "They devoted themselves to the teaching of the Apostles and to the communal fellowship, to the breaking of bread and to prayers" (Acts 2:42). In the same way, Paul urges the faithful of Thessalonica to pray humbly, vigilantly, with perseverance and trust: "pray continually" (1 Thes 5:17). He also says: "Let the word of Christ with all its richness dwell in you. Teach and admonish one another in all wisdom, singing psalms, hymns, and spiritual songs to God with gratitude in your hearts" (Col 3:16). Finally, he recommends to the Ephesians: "In all of your prayers and entreaties, pray always in the Spirit. To that end, keep alert and always persevere in supplication for all the saints" (Eph 6:18).

The Christians in Jerusalem went to the Temple frequently to praise and bless the Lord (Lk 24:53). The early Church, just as in other times, prayed as a community with one heart and one soul, in union with its Lord and Spouse, and as such, it shared in the love of the Son for the Father, in accordance with the conciliar text (SC 7). Saint Augustine often said: "Christ and the Church are two in one flesh; that is why they are two in one single voice." The same Spirit who prayed through Jesus prays today through the Church, repeating in our hearts: "*Abba*, Father" (Rom 8:15).

Every day, united in spirit, they would assemble together in the temple. They would break bread in their homes and share their

> food with joyful and generous hearts as they praised God, and they were regarded with favor by all the people.   (Acts 2:46-47)

Until the 4th century, on Sundays and on the feasts of martyrs, the Christian community took part in an Office of prayer, mornings and evenings, under the guidance of its clergy. This Office consisted of readings from the Bible and psalms. Later on, the monks developed it into prayers to be recited at different hours of the day, the main ones being Lauds, Vespers, and the night Office, called Matins. They added Terce, Sext, and Nones to sanctify the course of the whole day. The clerics of the Mendicant Orders, who were mostly involved in preaching, would often miss the choral service. And so they carried with them an abbreviated version of the Office, hence the name *Breviary*. The clergy adopted the *Breviary* for the recitation of the Hours in private. After the Council of Trent in 1568, Pius V promulgated the *Roman Breviary*. Other innovations were made by different popes in the centuries that followed, the most important one being the reinstatement by Pius X of the weekly recitation of the 150 psalms. Pius XII made official a better translation of the psalms which was itself replaced by the revised version of the *Vulgate*. Just before Vatican II, John XXIII made small changes in the text in order to simplify it.

For a long time, devout Christians used to attend Friday Vespers.

The Eastern Churches also have a Divine Office during which hymns of great beauty and spiritual depth are sung.

> The Liturgy of the Hours, like other liturgical actions, is not something private but belongs to the whole body of the Church, which it manifests and influences.   (GI 20)

The Church is a holy nation with a sacred calling: it cannot follow its course nor carry out its mission of salvation without "the sacrifice of praise," "of eternal praise" (*laus perennis*). Its duty is to take up and spread everywhere on earth the eternal song of its Spouse, thus continuing "the work of human Redemption and perfect glorification of God" (SC 5). The eternal hymn of the Chosen ones in Heaven described in the Book of Revelation actually begins down here on earth. Our celebrations, in fact, herald the heavenly liturgy and give us a foretaste of it.

Those who have been baptized share in the priesthood of the only Priest; in union with Him, they offer up a spiritual worship. Wholly and substantially one with their Leader, they worship, love, and pray through Him and with Him. "Let us recognize our voices in Him and His voice in us" states Saint Augustine. The Spirit who inspired the prophets is still the driving force within the Church. The last words of the New Testament state it clearly: "The Spirit and the bride say, 'Come!' " (Rev 22:17). The Bride also calls out to her Beloved: "Amen. Come Lord Jesus!" (Rev 22:20). Those are the words that end the divine revelation.

With the *Liturgy of the Hours*, all the Churches in the East and the West, the North and the South carry on the prayer of the pilgrims walking towards their eternal dwelling and identifying more and more with their Savior.

Whenever the congregation prays and chants as it celebrates the liturgy, Christ is present among the faithful and speaks through them (SC 7). No matter how small it may be, the community embodies and represents the universal Church. It is both fraternal and hierarchic: fraternal, because it unites the hearts and minds; hierarchic, since it has a presider and it prays with its pastors. Is it not true that the brotherly life thrives on giving praise and praise builds brotherhood? This applies to any ecclesial community: the diocese, the parish, a religious order, or the family.

From the beginning, the early Christians had set specific times for their prayers, following in the Jewish tradition. The Acts of the Apostles shows the disciples, like the Jews, praying three times a day: in the morning, around noon, and in the evening (Acts 3:1; 10:9).

The spiritual masters of the day, such as Tertullian and Saint Cyprian, proposed this demanding ideal. Liturgical prayer has always included reading the Bible and singing psalms.

The excellence of Christian prayer lies in this, that it shares in the very love of the only-begotten Son for the Father and in that prayer which the Son put into words in his earthly life and which still continues unceasingly in the name of the whole human race and for its salvation, throughout the universal Church and in all its members.　(GI 7)

5

VATICAN II AND THE REFORM

The Fathers of the Council had to find a solution to a serious problem. Since many clerics had a poor understanding of Latin, they no longer considered the Office as prayer meant to sanctify the course of the day. Many priests recited the *Breviary* without giving any thought to the meaning of the Hours. Some would even recite the entire Office in the morning, including Compline. For many of them, instead of being a source of spiritual enrichment, the Office had become a chore they had to do to avoid committing a mortal sin. The directions were complicated and often incomprehensible. Why, for instance, were Vespers—an evening prayer—to be said before dinner during Lent? It made no sense.

The *Breviary* had been devised for monks. Today's priests, involved as they are in pastoral ministry, lead a very different life from that of monks. As mentioned previously, Pius V, after the Council of Trent, had made numerous changes in the Office, and Pius XII and John XXIII were the last to enact improvements. Clearly, the Fathers of the Council were faced with an enormous task, and they were far from unanimous on the subject. Subsequently, the various committees responsible for carrying out the directives that had been laid down did a remarkable job in preparing the Divine Office that would be approved by Paul VI on November 1, 1970.

The result of their work can be found in *Sacrosanctum Concilium*, the "Constitution on the Sacred Liturgy," in chapter 4, numbers 83-101, which deal with the Divine Office.

The beginning of the chapter approaches the question in an admirable theological and spiritual perspective. The Divine Office is the work of Christ Who came down to earth to carry on with the eternal praise He offers up to the Father; He has entrusted the Church, His Spouse, with the mission of continuing His prayer day and night, from the beginning to the end of time. Those who have been given such a mission "stand before the throne of God in the name of our Mother the Church" (SC 85). By virtue of their baptismal vocation, all Christians, especially religious communities, take part in the prayer of the glorious Christ. Priests do it by virtue of their ministry.

The next paragraph is of particular importance to priests in active ministry. Saint Paul urges the faithful to pray "unremittingly," for only the Lord can ensure that their apostolic work will be effective. The reform aims precisely at providing ministers and other members of the Church, be they lay people or members of a religious order, an Office that will foster their inner life and energize their ministry or apostolic action (SC 86-87). The Apostles had already clearly defined the vocation of ordained ministers: to devote themselves to praying and serving the Word (Acts 6:4). The Council left it up to the Monastic Orders to make their own reform in accordance to their tradition.

It is established as a fundamental principle that the Office must sanctify the course of the day and thus find again "the truth of time," (*veritas temporis*). Two Hours are devoted to this, Lauds, the morning prayer, and Vespers, the evening prayer, in accord with the sacred tradition of the universal Church. Lauds and Vespers are the two poles of the daily Office and constitute the main Hours (GI 29). "There was evening and morning," such is the rhythm found in the Book of Genesis.

Compline provides a brief elevation for the soul, the last prayer after the activities and strains of the day, just before resting for the night. Night Prayer consists of only one psalm.

Prime is no longer prayed, but the middle hours remain: Midmorning (terce), Midday (sext) and Midafternoon (nones), particularly for the Monastic Orders, but for individuals, one is allowed to choose only one of these hours. Sext seems to offer the perfect opportunity to turn to God in the midst of daily worries.

Finally, another appreciable modification, the Hour called Matins in the choral celebration remains the nighttime praise, but it is adapted in such a way that it can be said at any time of the day in the personal celebration; furthermore, it has fewer psalms but longer readings, mostly from the Bible (SC 90).

The *Liturgy of the Hours* aims at sanctifying time by following the rhythm of the day and of the year; it must permeate the course of our lives. Day after day, from the beginning of Advent until the end of the annual cycle, the liturgy allows us to better experience the mysteries of the Lord and the lives of the Saints. It extends to every moment of the day "the center and apex of the whole life of the Christian community" (GI 12).

The liturgy thus fits into time and its passing as the week and the year unfold. Furthermore, the Office, not only prepares and completes, but also enriches the celebration of the Eucharist.

Thanks to the *Liturgy of the Hours*, the Church is present before the Lord every moment and everywhere in the world, fulfilling its precept of constant prayer. In practice, while recognizing that modern man is very busy, it is a reminder that he needs to collect his thoughts at given moments.

By its very nature and primarily, this prayer pertains to the bishop and his ordained ministers, but it also applies to all of God's people. That is why Vatican II encourages the faithful to take part in the great ecclesial prayer, individually or communally, at least on special occasions. It is not reserved to ordained ministers, but belongs to the members of religious communities and to *all* Christians.

Priests have the duty, not only to recite the Divine Office, but also to educate the Christian community so that it will perpetuate Jesus' prayer by proclaiming the wonders of God. Isn't that precisely the service of prayer?—"the people whom I formed for Myself so that they may proclaim My praise" (Isa 43:21).

Unfortunately, the custom of Friday Vespers has been lost in many places. Limiting the liturgy to the celebration of the Eucharist amounts to impoverishing it. On the contrary, given the simpler existing rubrics, we would enrich it by promoting the celebration of Lauds and Vespers in parishes or other Christian communities. Not to mention the fact that the new Code of Canon Law invites lay people to take part in the *Liturgy of the Hours* whenever possible (Can. 1174, 2).

The Council's directives offer this new opportunity to the Christian family since it is one of the groups to which the communal celebration of the *Divine Office* is recommended.[6]

In accordance with the wishes expressed by Vatican II, the new Office has become "a true source of devotion" and "food for our personal prayer." In addition, it should be a source of spiritual joy for ordained ministers. The presentation of the psalms with titles and new antiphons, the variety and richness of the biblical readings and hymns, the silent pauses, etc., these are all the

---

[6] John Paul II, Apostolic Exhortation *Familiaris Consortio*.

different means used to ensure that "the spirit be more easily in tune with the voices."

It's extraordinary to think that in the entire world, from the Pope down to the laity, the same words have been spoken for so many centuries. It is a communion through time and space.

6

THE PSALMS

To be able to recite the psalms in one's own language is a real inspiration. Before the reform, Christians would recite a few in Latin, such as *De Profundis*, out of sheer habit. When they first read them in translation, it was a revelation for many, an amazing discovery. These songs of praise were the prayer of Abraham's descendants, our ancestors in the faith. Some of the psalms are attributed to King David. The 150 psalms were collected in one book and used on the great days of worship, and for processions and pilgrimages. They bear witness to the history of the chosen people—the history of Israel is embedded in the text of the psalms.

It's wonderful to think that Jesus Himself addressed His Father with those same words the Holy Spirit had inspired, that He recited them in His house in Nazareth, at the synagogue, in the Temple of the Holy City, when He prayed alone, and even on the Cross. Throughout the centuries, Christians have chanted psalms in cathedrals and monasteries. The Fathers from the East and from the West—Saint Augustine in particular—have written commentaries on them. Saint Jerome translated them in Latin for the *Vulgate*. For the past 2000 years, monks and ordained ministers

have used the psalms in prayer. Every day, they
sustain the piety of religious people everywhere.
They are now part of the Liturgy of the Word; the
post-conciliar reform has introduced the Respon-
sorial Psalm that follows the first reading. Above
all, the psalms form the very framework of the
Liturgy of the Hours.

Hebrew poetry is based on the rhythm of two or
three stressed syllables. It is mainly characterized
by parallel verses: the second verse takes up the
first one in different words. Here is a typical example to help us better understand:

If the LORD does not build the house,
those who construct it labor in vain.
If the LORD does not guard the city,
those who keep watch over it do so in vain.

(Ps 127:1)

The parallelism may also be based on the
antithesis of the verses:

Those who go forth weeping,
carrying the seeds to be sown,
will return with shouts of joy,
carrying their sheaves.   (Ps 126:6)

Finally, the parallelism may lie in the synthesis
of the verses, whereby the second verse explains
the thought behind the first one:

Sing to the Lord a new song.   (Ps 98:1)

Sing joyfully to the Lord all the earth.

(Ps 98:4)

Hebrew poetry often uses alliterations, dialogues, and choruses.

The Semites are not afraid to use powerful images. They speak of the face of God, of His hands, His arms, His eyes, ears and mouth, of His breath. Their God is a concrete, living God. The Lord has remained for us a shield, a rock, a fortress, and a citadel.

The psalmist invents descriptive expressions that recur, like the following one:

> But you, O Lord, are a merciful and compassionate God,
> slow to anger and abounding in kindness and faithfulness. (Ps 86:15)

The psalmist is a true poet:

> You are clothed in majesty and splendor,
> wrapped in light as in a robe.
> You have stretched out the heavens like a tent;
> You have established Your palace upon the waters.
> You make the clouds serve as Your chariot;
> You ride forth on the wings of the wind.
> (Ps 104:1-3)

Inspired by the Spirit, the author also uses daring words to express God's goodness and mercy:

> For His anger lasts for only a moment,
> while His goodwill endures for a lifetime.
> (Ps 30:6)

Psalm 103 is a magnificent hymn to divine goodness:

As a father has compassion for his children,
so the LORD has compassion for those who
 fear Him.   (v. 13)

It is important to remember that there are different categories of psalms. In order to understand some of them, we must place them in their historical context. Many psalms refer to the founding event that was for the Jewish people its exodus from Egypt, such as psalm 114A:

When Israel came out of Egypt.   (v. 1)

Why do you skip like rams, O mountains,
and like lambs of the flock, O hills?
                                       (v. 6)

In 587, Nebuchadnezzar and his hordes lay waste the Holy City and its Temple:

They set upon it with their axes
as if it were a thicket of trees.
And then, with hatchets and hammers,
they bludgeoned all the carved work.
They set Your sanctuary ablaze;
they razed and defiled the dwelling place of
 Your Name.   (Ps 74:5-7)

Exiled in a foreign land, the Israelites lament their country in lyrical tones:

By the waters of Babylon
we sat down and wept
when we remembered Zion.
There on the poplars
we hung up our harps.   (Ps 137:1-2)

They hum happy tunes upon their return from exile:

> When the Lord brought home the captives to
>   Zion,
> we seemed to be dreaming.
> Our mouths were filled with laughter
> and our tongues with songs of joy.
>
> (Ps 126:1-2)

Whenever we recite these psalms, we relive the history of Israel.

The psalms are classified in major categories according to theme.

Psalms 113 to 118 make up what is known as the "Little Hallel," and psalms 120-136 are the "Great Hallel." They are songs of praise and they hold a special place in the liturgy of great feasts. Jesus recited these psalms during the Last Supper on the Jewish Passover. Some of the verses are very moving:

> How can I repay the Lord
> for all the good He has done for me?
> I will lift up the cup of salvation.
>
> (Ps 116:12-13)

With an anguished heart, Jesus continues:

> The bonds of death encompassed Me;
> the snares of the netherworld held Me tightly.
>
> (Ps 116:3)

And then:

> All the nations surrounded Me.

They surrounded Me on every side;
in the name of the L ord I overcame them.

(Ps 118:10-11)

The Master proclaims the Lord's infinite blessings towards His people by repeating twenty-six times the refrain from Psalm 136:

For His love endures forever!

The fifteen psalms (120-134) that the children of Israel sang during their pilgrimage to Jerusalem are referred to as the Psalms of Ascent. When we recite them, let's think of the people who sang them so many times, and let's remember that we are also pilgrims ascending to the heavenly heights:

I lift my eyes to the mountains;
from where will I receive help?   (Ps 121:1)

On arriving at their destination, the pilgrims would sing out all together:

And finally our feet are standing
at your gates, O Jerusalem.
Jerusalem is built as a city
that is firmly found together in unity.

(Ps 122:2-3)

In the messianic psalms, Christians recognize the Son of God Who came down to earth. Each Friday, at dawn and in the evening, the Church listens to the Father Who speaks to His Beloved:

You are My Son;
this day I have begotten You.   (Ps 2:7)

Yours is royal dignity in the day of Your birth;
in holy splendor, before the daystar,
like the dew, I have begotten You. (Ps 110:3)

Psalm 72 announces the coming of the Kings to Bethlehem to pay homage to the newborn, and Psalm 45 extols God's covenant with humanity. They also paint the picture of the Good Shepherd:

The Lord is my shepherd
there is nothing I shall lack.
He leads me to tranquil streams.   (Ps 23:1-2)

The Christian tradition sees in many psalms (22, 38, 40, 69) the suffering and anguish of Christ during His painful passion and agony:

They put gall in My food,
and in My thirst they gave Me vinegar to
drink.   (Ps 69:22)

On the Cross, Jesus utters the words of Psalm 22 that gives very striking details of the humiliations He is subjected to:

All who see Me jeer at Me;
they sneer in mockery and toss their heads.
(v. 8)

Finally, many psalms (4, 16, 17, 28) clearly allude to Christ's Resurrection:

He has helped me, and I exult;
then with My song I praise Him.   (Ps 28:7)

There are also seven psalms on the theme of penance, the best known of which are *Miserere* (Ps 51) and *De Profundis* (Ps 130).

The Book of Psalms holds a prominent place in the liturgy; like the people of the Old Covenant, the Church lives in the midst of suffering and persecution, but also in joy and hope, until the final victory. That is why the psalms are not recited as an individual prayer, but in union with Christ and His Church, with all our brothers and sisters, Saints and sinners, with the humble, the suffering, and the dying.

In his exquisite Latin, Saint Augustine wrote: *Psalmus vox totius Christi, capitis et corporis,* "The psalms are the voice of the whole Christ, the head and the body."

The psalms, the prayer of a people, became Jesus' prayer and today, Jesus' prayer has become the prayer of the Church.

Many of the psalms will acquire a new flavor if we recite them in union with the Lord Jesus, taking His feelings upon ourselves. Once again, the Bishop of Hippo says it best: "Try not to say anything without Him and He will say nothing without you." The psalms shape our souls after the soul of Jesus Who recited them in every situation of His life. "The christological interpretation was never limited to those psalms that are considered as messianic, but extends to many others" (GI 109). Hence the importance of grasping their meaning as a whole.

The imprecatory verses may surprise us but they indicate in their own way the violence and harshness of humanity; they are the cries of those who were persecuted. Basic differences are not always resolved through understanding. "It's as if these psalms were meant to remind us that believing implies a constant struggle between God's holiness and the sins of the world, between good and evil, light and darkness." [7]

The psalms are also the prayer of "social outcasts and prisoners, of those who suffer, who are ill or dying." We can therefore recite them as the prayer of a missionary Church, persecuted by its enemies, a Church on a journey, and as the prayer of all the men and women in the world.

The psalms are not merely texts to be read, nor are they prayers in prose; they are poems of praise that express, "a joyful spirit and a loving heart" (GI 104), admiration, thanksgiving, and the cries of God's people.

The typographic setting of the psalms makes it easier to understand them. The presentation of each psalm includes:

- a title that suggests its general meaning;
- a short sentence, almost always from the New Testament, which stresses its christological value;
- an antiphon which is the key to the psalm, so to speak, since it brings out its central idea or how it relates to the feast being celebrated.

---

[7] Three psalms do not appear in the *Liturgy of the Hours*, psalms 58, 83 and 109, because of their particularly vehement character. Besides 147 psalms, the Office includes 39 canticles from the Old Testament and 9 from the New Testament.

At the beginning, the antiphon introduces the psalm; at the end, it summarizes its meaning.

Tradition recommends reciting *Glory to the Father* after the psalm. It brings to the prayers from the Old Testament "a quality of praise linked to a christological and trinitarian interpretation" (GI 123). "The *Liturgy of the Hours* must be seen as the ideal time to learn to pray, especially because of the psalms." [8]

There are three ways to chant the psalms:

- in a sequence, reading the verses or singing them from beginning to end;
- with two choirs alternating the singing of verses or stanzas;
- using the responsive form, that is by repeating the antiphon or a verse after each stanza. This way is particularly suited to psalms 8, 46, 67 and 147, as well as to the invitatory psalms.

The sapiential and historical psalms may be read by either one person or the entire congregation, whereas the thanksgiving hymns and psalms are usually sung by all or alternately.

To help the faithful understand the psalms and turn them into Christian prayer, the General Introduction suggests that they be followed by a psalmodic prayer. In accordance with ancient tradition, this prayer makes the psalm more relevant to Christians by revealing the mystery of Christ.

---

[8] *Instrumentum laboris*, Roman synod of 2008, n° 34.

Let us apply the Council's guidelines and help Christians to rediscover the meaning of the psalms and the prayer within them.

All those who might be unable to read the whole Bible will find a comprehensive summary of it in this little book [of psalms].
(Martin Luther)

7

THE LITURGICAL CYCLES

The liturgical cycles are woven into the cycles of the universe but they do not close in on themselves; while constantly recurring, they open on to the future and the glorious return of Christ. Our liturgy follows the rhythm of life, with its daily, weekly, and annual cycles.

The first, the daily cycle, is centered on the celebration of the Eucharist. With its seven Hours, the Divine Office invites us to come to God seven times a day. Each Hour is a break in our hectic day. We can even interrupt our sleep to sanctify the night with Matins. We shall discuss in this chapter the significance of each Hour.

As mentioned above, the *Liturgy of the Hours* contributes to sanctifying the day; it is thus strongly recommended to celebrate each Hour at the designated time, in other words, to respect "the proper of time" as much as possible (GI 11).

Sunday, the day of the Resurrection of the Lord and thus a day of vital importance, begins the week. The First Day brings us to the following Sunday, which the ancient authors often referred to as the Eighth Day, or the day beyond. The day of the Lord is also the day of the Church, the day of the Eucharist. The psalms for Sundays are chosen for their messianic and paschal meaning. For instance, Psalm 63 expresses our desire to meet the Lord as soon as the day breaks. The Canticle of Creation, from the three young men in the blazing fire, rises as a majestic symphony exalting the greatness of the Creator, while Psalm 150 conveys the joy that the Saints in heaven feel at having overcome evil. On the following Sundays, Psalm 118 evokes Jesus' victory on Easter morning and Psalm 93 describes again the greatness of God "covered in power and splendor," ruling over heaven and earth. The Sunday Lauds end with one of the three traditional psalms that crown the celebration, *Laudate*, "Give Praise," Psalms 148, 149 and 150. For Vespers, Psalm 110 *(The Lord Says to My Lord)* shows the glorious Messiah, king and priest, Whom the Father begets in all His dazzling holiness and to Whom He gives the scepter of strength to govern all nations. Next, Psalm 114 extols the wonders that accompanied the liberation of the Jewish people from Egypt and the crossing of the Red Sea. Then, the bridal song of the Lamb lifts our hearts towards the Blessed City. Both 118, the psalm of triumph, and 23, the psalm of the Good Shepherd, are recited at the middle hour.

In the weekly cycle, Friday's liturgy refers to the Passion and Death of Christ. Every Friday at Lauds, Psalm 51 reminds us that we are sinners and urges us to imitate David's repentance so that we can delight in the "joy of being saved." Psalm 21, which Jesus prayed on the Cross, as well as many others that are part of the Office of Readings, herald the Passion of the Suffering Servant.

The Saturday Office discreetly alludes to the Mother of Jesus, as do the praises, intentions, and prayers of the first and third Saturdays of the month.

Starting with Advent, the story of salvation unfolds in a great annual cycle; at its very center, we celebrate the death of our Lord and His Resurrection on Easter. This is the first mystery and the heart of the liturgical year which consists of two cycles: the cycle of Incarnation with its two poles, Christmas and Epiphany, and the cycle of Redemption, also with two poles, Resurrection and Pentecost.

Each year, until the feast of Christ the King, the *Liturgy of the Hours*, through its readings, hymns, and psalms, gives us the opportunity to relive the mystery of Christ, from humanity's long wait for the Messiah until His glorious return.

Concurrently, the cycle of days dedicated to the Saints and the Mother of our Savior allows us to venerate the Virgin Mary and a luminous host of heroes of saintliness. There are many Marian feasts, and Vatican II teaches us that the liturgy is the best way to pay homage to Mary. The calendar also brings back every year the memory of our brothers and sisters who have gone before us: Joseph, John the Baptist, Peter and Paul,

Apostles, martyrs, founders of churches or religious institutions, doctors, mystics, and humble servants of God. While glorifying God, the source of all holiness, these feasts help us to discover models and learn a little bit of the Church's history. The cycle of the Saints reaches its highest point on All Saints Day with the Gospel of the Beatitudes and a vision from Revelation: it shows a vast crowd "of all nations, races, peoples and languages standing before the Throne and the Lamb." Bernanos was right when he wrote: "Our Church is the Church of saints."

On feast days especially, the choice of psalms is often based on their Christological meaning, and antiphons taken from these psalms are frequently used to throw light on this meaning.   (GI 109)

8

THE MORNING PRAYER OF PRAISE

We call it the morning Office, but we could just as well refer to it as the morning praise, Lauds, from the Latin *laudes*, as this prayer is called in the monastic tradition.

This hour sanctifies the beginning of the day. As we get up, we contemplate nature rising from its sleep and admire it: "The heavens proclaim the glory of God; the firmament shows forth the work of His hands" (Ps 19:2). Before going to work or undertaking our daily tasks, let us collect our thoughts and strike up a chant to the Lord. Let us break the silence of the night and sing the praises of He Who created heaven and earth and makes "the great lamp" that lights our universe. "You are my refuge and my fortress, my God in whom I place my trust," says Psalm 92.

This hour also evokes the Resurrection of Jesus, the Light of the World, Who triumphed over the shades of death. "After He had risen from the dead early on the first day of the week," writes Mark (16:9). "At daybreak on the first day of the week," writes Luke for his part (24:1).

Already in the third century, the bishop of Carthage, Saint Cyprian, would say: "There should be prayer in the morning, so that the resurrection of the Lord may be celebrated by morning prayer."

A liturgist has drawn attention to the fact that the morning Hour celebrates the Resurrection of Christ, the resurrection of creation, and that of the Church. As a result, the texts of the Office at dawn, especially on Sundays, present the risen Savior, and the theme of light permeates this Hour completely. The Church acclaims the Lord, "the dawn from on high will break upon us" (Lk 1:78).

In general, it is an invitatory psalm that leads us into the morning prayer. Psalm 95 invites the congregation to "sing out with joy to the Lord" and "extol Him with our songs." If appropriate, Psalms 24, 67, and 100 can replace Psalm 95.

If time permits, it is best to repeat the antiphon after each stanza, thereby proclaiming the theme of the feast or the mystery commemorated by the liturgy. From the very beginning of the Office, the repeated antiphon rings out like the coming of good tidings.

Then comes the hymn that emphasizes the theme of the Hour, the particular feast or liturgical time. Many of the hymns are very poetic and beautifully written.

The central part of the Office, the psalmody, follows the hymn. The first psalm is usually a morning prayer that expresses our thirst for God, our trust in Him and our supplication. Here are some examples:

O LORD, at daybreak You hear my voice;
at daybreak I bring my petition before You
and await Your reply.   (Ps 5:4)

As the deer longs for running streams,
so my soul longs for You, O God.   (Ps 42:2)

Awake lyre and harp!
I will awaken the dawn.   (Ps 108:3)

Incline Your ear, O LORD, and answer me,
for I am poor and needy.
Grant me a sign of Your favor.   (Ps 86:1, 17)

Through the canticle, always from the Old Testament, we join our prayers to those of the patriarchs and prophets of the First Covenant who, in the presence of the Lord, openly displayed their anguish and trust, their worship and hope. It is good for us to pray together with Isaiah, Jeremiah, Ezekiel, with the Saints of long ago, like David, Ann, Tobias, Judith, and Ben Sirach the Sage. Just as our fathers in the faith did, we await the salvation that comes from God.

The last psalm of the morning prayer—always one of praise—is in tune with the specific character of the Hour. Together with all living things in the universe, the people of ancient Jerusalem and all the nations of the world, with the Angels and the chosen of the Heavenly City, let us glorify our Creator and Savior:

O LORD, our LORD,
how glorious is Your name in all the earth!

(Ps 8)

All you peoples, clap your hands,
shout to God with cries of gladness. (Ps 47)

Praise the Lord, O Jerusalem!
Glorify your God, O Zion!   (Ps 147:12)

Zechariah's Canticle is both the heart and the climax of the morning Hour. When John the Baptist is born, the saintly old man foresees the coming of the Savior, Sun of justice Who already appears on the horizon and is coming down to us (the next chapter will comment on this).

The prayers of intercession are both praises and petitions. These prayers, which have found their place again in the celebration of the Eucharist, are more than intercessions in the *Liturgy of the Hours*; they also have a laudatory aspect, in keeping with the very nature of this Hour.

Early in the morning, we lift our hearts to the merciful Father by reciting or singing the Sunday prayer.

Finally, the presider gathers the intentions of the congregation as he recites the collect. Finally, he dismisses the participants with "May God be with you" and his blessing.

According to Saint Basil, "in the morning hour we give praise to dedicate the first movements of the soul and spirit to God, so that we will not undertake anything before having rejoiced at the thought of God, as it is written 'I groan as I think of God; my spirit grows faint as I meditate on Him. . . . I will call to mind Your wonders in the past' " (Ps 77:4, 12).

Let all the faithful, men and women, as soon as they awaken, before they do anything else, wash their hands and pray to God; after that, they can go about their daily business.

(Saint Hippolytus, *Apostolic Tradition*)

9

ZECHARIAH'S CANTICLE

As the Angel had announced to Mary, Elizabeth gave birth to a son at an advanced age. Eight days later, the newborn was circumcised and given the name John, *Yôhânân* in Hebrew, which means "the Lord grants a favor."

Before all who were present, the father, filled with the Holy Spirit, prophesied:

Blessed be the Lord, the God of Israel,
for He has visited His people and redeemed
  them.
He has raised up a horn of salvation for us
from the house of His servant David.

(Lk 1:68-69)

Zechariah proclaims the visit of the Lord King promised to David. And indeed, the Savior is in their midst, inside the womb of the Virgin from Nazareth who has come to give a hand to her cousin Elizabeth, John the Baptist's mother.

God had sworn an oath to David: "One of your own descendants I will place on your throne" (Ps 132:11b). According to Gabriel's promise, Jesus, Son of the Almighty, will inherit David's throne and reign eternally on the house of Jacob (Lk 1:32).

Humble and powerful, Jesus will deliver His people from their enemies and reveal "His Father's infinite mercy. He will seal the New Covenant with His blood.

The Lord had also solemnly pledged to Abraham, the father of all believers, that his descendants would be as numerous as the stars in the sky and the grains of sand in the sea. They are now the Church, which is rooted in the race of Israel and which brings together the nations on earth, of all languages and origins. Out of this throng, Jesus will create a royal and priestly people for the Father's glory.

In the second half of Zechariah's Canticle, the old man greets his son, little John the Baptist, prophet of the Almighty, the messenger who was sent to prepare the way for the coming King; his voice will shout in the desert: "A voice cries out: In the wilderness prepare the way of the LORD" (Is 40:3).

Zechariah's son will indeed point to the Lamb of God, the Spouse of the Covenant.

Let us thus rejoice, for Jesus is David's Offspring, the messianic Gift, Sun of Justice, Morning Star, dazzling Light from above that shines upon those who are lost in the darkness and shows the path to peace.

In the past, the Lord has redeemed the people of Israel from slavery through many a wonderful intervention. And yet, the ancient feast of Passover is just an image of the new one, the true passage. The new Passover is much more than the exodus from Egypt and the crossing of the

Red Sea. This time, Jesus leads His people to the Promised Land, the true homeland, by accomplishing miracles and new wonders.

The Light that appeared on that blessed night in Bethlehem—the Son of God among us—will shine brightly on Easter night and overcome the shadows of sin and death. "I am the Resurrection and the Life" proclaims Jesus. Prince of Peace, He will reunite the scattered children of God and reconcile them with Himself and with His Father.

Zechariah uses the style and words of the Old Testament, but his Canticle heralds the advent of a New Covenant.

Thus, at the beginning of each day, after having praised the Creator for a vast and beautiful universe and all its blessings, the children of the Church repeat the old man's hymn to thank the Father Who gave us His only Son and resurrected Him at dawn on Easter Sunday.

Throughout the new day, as the Precursor did, we shall walk before God in justice and saintliness and, by our work, prepare for the return of the Star up above, sign of salvation and divine tenderness.

Zechariah's Canticle and its antiphon are at the heart of the Office and deserve the same "solemnity and dignity" accorded the proclamation of the Gospel (GI 138).

10

THE EVENING PRAYER

The sun has completed its journey across the sky and is now slowly setting behind the mountain tops, leaving behind its fiery glow; another day has gone. The Christian community gathers once more, for the time has come to thank the Lord for all His blessings of the day. It's the Hour of Vespers, from the Latin *vesper*, "evening." A prayer of thanksgiving rises to God.

Let us say together the words of Psalm 141:

May my prayer be like incense before You,
the lifting up of my hands like the evening
     sacrifice.   (Ps 141:2)

It is the *sacrificium vespertinum*, the "evening sacrifice," the "sacrifice of praise."

Among the Jews, on the evening before the Sabbath and other feasts, the celebration begins with the ritual lighting of the lamps. In some Churches, especially in the East, the lamps are lit to the singing of psalms, such as Psalm 119:

Your word is a lamp for my feet
and a light to my path.   (Ps 119:105)

By joining our voices to those of the Eastern Churches (GI 39), we acclaim Christ with a magnificent hymn:

". . . joy-giving light of holy glory, born of the immortal, heavenly Father, holy and blessed,

Jesus Christ; now that we have come to the setting of the sun and seen the evening star, we sing in praise of the Father and the Son and the Holy Spirit as God. . . ."

Roman liturgy, for its part, has maintained the ritual of the Service of Light only on the night before Easter, when the new flame and the paschal candle are blessed and Easter is announced with the *Exultet*. The altar and the congregation are incensed during the singing of the *Magnificat*.

When the sun goes down and the day wanes, we must pray. Christ is the true Sun, the real Day. (Saint Cyprian)

In the Temple of Jerusalem, the High Priest offered the ritual sacrifice at the end of each day. But the only real sacrifice of the New Covenant is the sacrifice of Jesus Who, with open arms on the Cross, gave Himself for the world's salvation. And so, the Hour of Vespers reminds us each evening of that great gesture of love on Good Friday.

Psalm 136 is recited on Holy Thursday. It is a paschal hymn that relates all the wonders the Lord accomplished for Israel. Jesus Himself said it with His Apostles during His Last Supper. None of the Lord's blessings can compare with the Eucharist, sacrament of the Passion and sacrifice of Jesus.

The reform of Vatican II limited the evening prayer to two psalms and one canticle from the

New Testament (instead of five psalms). It was a very fortunate innovation, since the canticle gives Vespers a typically christological character: Jesus is at the center of the verses taken from the Letters from Saint Paul or from Revelation.

The Sunday psalms, according to tradition, emphasize the mystery of the Resurrection. The first one, Psalm 110, depicts the glorious Messiah, King and Priest, Ruler of all nations. Next, Psalm 114 exalts the Lord for all the wonders He performed to liberate His people from slavery in Egypt. Psalm 115 glorifies the One and Only God, higher than all idols, blessing His servants.

Psalm 111 describes the Lord's resounding works, and Psalm 112 proclaims the bliss of the righteous who shine like a light in the darkness. Isn't Jesus Himself one of the righteous?

The congregation sings the Hallelujah of the chosen who, bursting with joy, celebrate the union of the victorious sacrificial Lamb with His glowingly beautiful Bride (Rev 19). During Lent, the New Testament canticle taken from Peter's First Letter invokes the Lord's Servant Who, through His suffering and Passion, heals our wounds.

During the week, we come across many psalms of thanksgiving (136, 138, 144, etc.) that help us in giving God our own thanks.

Worthy of notice is a poem by the psalmist who describes the wedding of the King—"the most handsome of men" to the Church—"the king will desire your beauty" surrounded by her companions in the bridal procession (Ps 45:3, 12).

On the first Friday of the month, Psalm 41 is the source of our meditation on the humiliations that the Savior suffered when He was betrayed and abandoned.

At the heart of Vespers, the Church repeats with Our Lady her beautiful words of thanksgiving. There is nothing better than the *Magnificat* to express gratitude (see next chapter).

The rest of the Hour follows the same pattern as the morning prayer.

In Ambrosian liturgy, Vespers on a feast day ends with a procession to the baptismal font. This ritual, rich in symbolism, could be practiced again under certain circumstances, for example during Holy Week.

Shouldn't we reinstate Sunday Vespers in their rightful place in Christian worship? We would then rediscover the meaning of Sunday.

> Pastors of souls should see to it that the principal hours, especially Vespers, are celebrated in common in church on Sundays and on the more solemn feasts. (SC 100)

11

THE CANTICLE OF MARY

Every day, late in the afternoon, the Church sings Mary's Canticle. Let us try to understand the meaning and beauty of this hymn.

According to Jewish custom, a girl engaged to be married would write a poem for her wedding. That is how she expressed her happiness. She probably took her inspiration from traditional popular songs. The wedding guests would respond by repeating the chorus, clapping their hands, and laughing. Family, friends, and especially the spouses thus showed openly their collective rejoicing.

On the day of the Annunciation, Miriam, as she was called in Aramaic, her native tongue, says "yes" to the Angel's request. Her answer is given freely, spontaneously, and lovingly in the name of humanity. Without this generous "yes" on the part of the Virgin from Nazareth, God could not have carried out His plan for salvation. With her consent, everything becomes possible. God is made flesh and He inaugurates a New Covenant with us. At that moment, the simple girl is transformed into the dwelling place of the Only Son, the Ark of the Covenant.

Without delay, carrying her treasure inside, the Virgin leaves for the village of Ain Karim, across the mountains of Judea. When she arrives, she is greeted by Elizabeth with these words: "Blessed are you among women and blessed is the fruit of your womb." Just like all the girls engaged to be married, Mary breaks out in a song of praise and thanksgiving.

On her journey, she has prayed and meditated "in her heart" on the psalms and the prophecies. She now reinterprets the Scriptures, giving them an entirely new meaning. In the footsteps of Judith, the brave woman who defeated Holofernes, The Mother of God exalts, "You are the God of the lowly, the helper of the oppressed, the support of the weak, the protector of the forsaken, the savior of those who have lost all hope" (Jud 9:11).

Mary's heart, as did Anne's heart when Samuel was born, rejoices in her Savior, already present in her bosom.

God's promise to Abraham is fulfilled in Mary, as is Isaiah's prophecy that a virgin would conceive a son Emmanuel; in her is sealed the Covenant between the Lord and His people.

Our Lady of the Visitation sings the Beatitudes before her Son, for she proclaims blessed the poor, the afflicted, those who are hungry and those who are persecuted. In fact, the *Magnificat* has been called the Gospel of Mary. The humble servant herself will be exalted throughout the centuries.

The Canticle of Mary also foreshadows The Book of Revelation. Indeed, it prophesies that the pharaohs and the powerful will be deposed and reduced to nothing, while God's servants will be glorified in the Heavenly City.

Our daily *Magnificat* echoes the very first one and Mary's eternal *Magnificat*.

At the end of each day, the Church collects itself and takes up again this great Marian prayer to thank the Savior Who looks upon the humility of His lowly servant, upon the poverty of His Church and all its servants (Lk 1:46-48) and sees them all as blessed.

The Church invites us to acknowledge, along with Mary, the power, holiness, and mercy of God:

The Mighty One has done great things for
   me,
and holy is His name.
His mercy is shown from age to age
to those who fear Him." (Lk 1:49-50)

All together, we give thanks to God Who sets free the poor and the oppressed and strikes down the arrogant and the persecutors. As He promised, the Almighty gave Abraham countless descendants and a first-born, Jesus Christ. Through Him, we united ourselves with the people of Israel, as Saint Paul writes. The Lord has also fulfilled His promise in regard to His Son Jesus and His servant Mary. Following Mary's example, the Church rejoices because it believes in the infallible Word and in a divine loyalty as unshakable as a rock. Mary's prayer echoes Abraham's joy and predicts Jesus' exultation as He reveals to the simple people the wisdom hidden from the wise men of this world. The Roman Directive *Liberty and Liberation*,[9] in a commentary on the *Magnificat*, states that Mary proclaims "the victory of divine Love and the liberation of the poor."

And so, the poem by the Virgin Mother which crowns the prayers of Israel is at the height of our own daily prayer. To offer praise or give thanks, nothing surpasses repeating the words of the woman who is the very model of the praying Church. In his Apostolic Exhortation on Marian worship, Paul VI writes that "the Canticle of the Virgin has become the prayer of the whole Church for all times." It is the echo on earth of the heavenly praise that Mary gives the Trinity.

We must approach the Canticle of Mary with the same solemn respect as we would the readings from the Gospel. Why not stand to sing it and make the Sign of the Cross before we begin? On important feast days, we could also incense the altar.

> *Therefore it is an excellent and beneficial custom, whose fragrance fills the Holy Church, to sing the Canticle of the Virgin every day at vespers. One can expect that a stronger fervor will be kindled in the souls*

---

[9] Congregation for the Doctrine of the Faith, March 22, 1986.

of the faithful if they often recall the Incarnation of the Lord, and that the frequent recollection of the example set by his Holy Mother will strengthen their virtue.

(Venerable Bede)

12

PRAYING BEFORE
RESTING FOR THE NIGHT

The sun has set. The world is shrouded in darkness. Human beings and animals alike settle into peaceful silence. In the night, we have an image of death.

Each day that fades away is a reminder of how brief life is. Scripture tells us that the devil, our enemy, shuns the light and lurks about in the shadows, looking for someone to devour. That is why Christians turn to God and place their trust in Him.

Before we rest for the night, we are urged to lift our hearts once again toward the Lord. Compline is the last prayer of the day, and it is said just before going to sleep, even after midnight, if it happens to be the case (GI 84). It is very short, but exceptionally rich and beautiful. Monks and cloistered nuns recite Compline before the long silence of the night. Lay people are also encouraged to celebrate this last Hour.

Night time is for silence and meditation. Everything invites us to collect our thoughts and let nothing disturb our meeting with God.

Jesus prayed at night; so did the Saints. The short prayer of Compline continues this tradition. Compline reminds us of Jesus resting in His sepulcher while waiting for the shining moment of His Resurrection. Just before dying, He committed His soul to God and He knew that God would not leave it among the dead, nor would He abandon His body in that place of corruption (Ps 16:10).

Compline begins with an examination of conscience followed by an act of repentance.

After the initial hymn comes a psalm, a different one each day of the week, one that underlines ideas specific to this Hour.

In the past, three psalms (4, 136, 91), borrowed from the monastic tradition, were recited on Sundays.

Nowadays on Saturdays, we thank the Lord with Psalm 4, for He lets us live in confidence (v. 9). To that is added the short psalm 134, a night greeting that the pilgrims addressed to the guardians of the Temple as they were leaving Jerusalem:

Come forth to bless the LORD,
all you servants of the LORD,
who minister throughout the night
in the house of the LORD.
Lift up your hands toward the sanctuary
and bless the LORD.   (Ps 134:1-2)

On Sundays, with Psalm 91, we pray to God as our refuge and citadel in the midst of temptation and all our troubles.

On Mondays, Tuesdays, and Wednesdays, Psalms 31, 86, 130, and 143 express perfectly our absolute trust in and our supplication to the Heavenly Father.

On Thursdays, David proclaims God as our heritage in Psalm 16. We shall never be forgotten in the throes of death and the grave. And for that, our hearts rejoice and our souls celebrate.

Finally, on Fridays, Psalm 88 conveys the feeling of abandonment that Jesus experienced during His Passion, the same as someone who feels weak and sick, close to death. The psalm expresses our deep anguish in the face of our last hour.

Thus, before going to sleep, we find comfort and hope in some verses from the Bible:

They shall see the Lord face to face and bear His name on their foreheads.

(Sunday, Rev 22:4)

Do not forsake us, Lord, our God.

(Friday, Jer 14:9)

We respond to this brief reading by repeating Jesus' dying words on the Cross: "Into your hands, O Lord, I commend My Spirit."

At the top of the Hour, we sing the third canticle found in Luke's Infancy Narrative. In the Temple in Jerusalem, a righteous and devout old man was waiting for the consolation of Israel, the promised Messiah. When Mary and Joseph came to present the Child, Simeon took Him in his arms and, inspired by the Spirit, he praised God for allowing him to see, before his death, "the Light of nations" and "the Glory of the chosen people." His song of gratitude refers back to Isaiah's prophecy on a Messiah of Light for all pagans to the ends of the earth and Glory for Abraham's race (Is 19:1-6).

Like Simeon, at the end of each day, we confess before the Lord that we are servants, "useless servants." Nonetheless, we can go in peace, for we have seen the signs of salvation and met the Lord. "Blessed the eyes that see what you see," says Jesus (Lk 10:23). By welcoming the Lord, we receive the true light and divine consolation.

The final prayer expresses our last wish. The prayers that close the Hour take up the fundamental themes of Compline: abandonment and peace, hope of resurrection, rest in the bosom of the Father of all mercies.

Since the Middle Ages, monks have been singing the *Salve Regina* at the end of the Office. The Church has kept alive the custom of singing (or reciting) a Marian antiphon as night begins.

With tender love, let us hail Mary, doorway to Heaven, sweet Mother of mercy and hope. We can now sleep peacefully until daylight returns; then we will once again bless God and serve Him with renewed generosity.

Jesus Christ, our Lord whose yoke is gentle and easy to bear, we place in your hands the burden of the day; grant us rest at your side.　　　　(Compline, Wednesday)

O Lord, may the splendor of your Resurrection shine brightly on us, so that we can escape the shadow of death and reach eternal light in your Kingdom.
(Compline, Friday)

13

LISTENING TO THE WORD OF GOD

Listening to the Word of God is an important way of praying, worshiping, and contemplating the mystery of the Holy Trinity. It is the rightful attitude of the disciple who is fascinated by his Master's wisdom, of the Church-Bride who listens reverently and joyfully to the voice of the Word, its Spouse.

Throughout the Office, chanting the psalms prepares the heart and mind to hear the proclamation of the sacred texts. The short readings are carefully chosen to suit the time in the liturgical cycle and the hour of the day.

It is possible to choose a longer passage from the Mass or other suitable readings. The General Introduction (58) gives clear instructions on the subject:

- the Gospels are excluded, since they are read during Mass throughout the year;
- the particular character of a given Sunday, Friday, or Hour must be taken into account;
- a text from the New Testament will be selected for the Evening Prayer.

It is not enough to listen, one must also meditate on the Word, better still, savor it. In doing so, we follow the example of Mary who sat at the Lord's feet and chose the best.

When celebrating with the people, one can also add a brief homily. It is up to the celebrant to distribute the bread of the Word to God's family. In some cases, reading a passage from a spiritual author can replace the homily.

Why not silently pause to better assimilate the divine message?

It is appropriate to answer God by interacting with Him. The congregation can thus sing a responsory hymn or respond briefly to the celebrant or sing any other canticle approved to this end (GI 42-49). The main thing is to receive and assimilate the Word which is the spirit and the life.

Listening to the Word is so important that the liturgy has kept an Office of Readings (*vigiliae matutinae*), Matins, which monks celebrate in the early hours of the morning. It is not just a reading or an intellectual exercise. One must receive, welcome, and celebrate the Word with a "unity of heart and voice" (GI 22).

By its very nature, the Hour of Matins has "the character of a night prayer" (Paul VI). Some Churches customarily open the most solemn of celebrations with a vigil, the Easter vigil being the most typical and the best known.

In the first centuries, Christians would pray as they waited for the return of the Lord, like the virgins in the parable who wait for a voice to ring out: "Keep watch and pray." This advice from Jesus is still valid today and for all times. The

Christmas and Pentecost vigils should really be celebrated more often and many others should be reinstated (GI 71). The 1975 edition of the *Roman Missal* includes the option of celebrating the vigil of Pentecost.

At the start of Matins, a hymn and three psalms create an atmosphere conducive to meditation and put us in the right mood to receive the message from the readings, which vary according to the liturgical time or feast of the day. The hymn is chosen from the night or day selections depending on the time of recitation (GI 61).

Then, the Church bestows upon us the dual treasure of the inspired Word and its age-old heritage. The liturgy of the Eucharist already provides us with the nourishment of the Word through a great variety of readings. The Divine Office completes this wealth of riches. It is in the Scriptures that we can get to know the Lord. Blaise Pascal wrote very wisely: "Only God speaks well about God." From year to year, the Word helps us to fathom the mystery of God and reveals His plan for our salvation.

Understanding the readings from the Bible requires some degree of initiation. It presupposes two things: an overall view of the history of the people of Israel and a little exegesis.

The Bible is composed of different literary genres. It is essential to know these genres in order to grasp the divine message hidden within. "To understand, we must distinguish between history and fables, and even between the substance of history and the images that are superimposed."[10] For instance, we can read the four chapters of the Book of Job as a hard luck story or as a text that reveals admirably God's mercy towards pagans. The introductions to the biblical readings are very well done and bring out the spiritual meaning of the texts. It is important that we practice *lectio divina* (see pp. 104-119).

The second reading of the Hour shows how the divine Word has been understood and lived out throughout the ages. From its inexhaustible treasure and with maternal wisdom, the Church chooses for its children "the finest excerpts from spiritual writers" (GI 55), ancient and recent. Cyprian, Augustine, Ambrose, Gregory of Nyssa, Bernard; the Cistercians of the XIIth century, Isaac of the Star, Baldwin of Ford, Aelred of Rievaulx all make us benefit from their Christian experience and their meditations on the Scriptures. To those can be added the names of Francis of Assisi, Francis de Sales, Paul VI, and so many others. It is surprising to note that, already in the early centuries, authors such as Origen, Irenaeus of Lyon, or Ignatius of Antioch understood the dogma of the Christian faith so well.

It is not without reason that ordained ministers are asked to "faithfully recite the Office of Readings" (GI 29).

---

[10] Louis Boyer, *Introduction to the Spiritual Life*, p. 52.

In the same spirit, a Roman Directive insists that the members of religious communities make the most of the riches hidden in the *Liturgy of the Hours*. So let us receive from the hands of our mother the Church these chosen texts like offerings at a banquet where we will find nourishment for our faith.

The responses that follow each reading aim at "turning what has been read into prayer and contemplation" (GI 169). They shed "a new light" on what has been read or heard. Quite often, they link the two Testaments.

On solemn celebrations and feasts, the Office can be prolonged by the vigil, that is by chanting three biblical canticles, in particular from the prophets: Isaiah, Jeremiah, etc. and the sapiential books: Proverbs, Wisdom, Sirach. These Canticles are in keeping with the ancient practices of different liturgies such as the Ambrosian and the Benedictine ones.

Then, a short passage from the Gospel is read. On ordinary Sundays, it announces the Resurrection by bringing out the paschal character of the day of the Lord; this follows the tradition of the Church of Jerusalem in the past. During Lent, the passage is about the Passion and Resurrection. The canticles and the passages from the Gospel for the vigils are listed at the end of each volume of the *Liturgy of the Hours*.

On Sundays and solemn celebrations, except during Lent, the Office of Readings ends with the singing of *Te Deum*, a magnificent hymn to the Almighty Father, His Son, and the Holy Spirit.

After the last prayer, the celebration ends with:

Let us praise the Lord.
And give Him thanks.

14

BESEECHING THE LORD

Saint Paul urges us to address the Lord with our supplications, prayers, and thanks for humankind (1 Tim 2:1-4). The reformed Divine Office suggests exactly these kinds of prayer. Indeed, asking with humility and trust is an authentic form of praise since it acknowledges the power and love of God. It is good to ask like a child who is sure of his Father's love or like a beggar in the presence of the merciful Almighty. Jesus tells us again and again that a persevering prayer is powerful and He assures us that the Heavenly Father will grant the Spirit—supreme gift—to those who shall ask Him.

In the morning and in the evening, the petitions which constitute the last part of the *Liturgy of the Hours* are divided into three parts:

- the requests or intercessions;
- the *Our Father;*
- the collect, or short final prayer.

The intercessions were fortunately reinstated in the two main liturgical Hours as they had been in the celebration of the Eucharist. In a very unique style, they combine praise and petitions, especially in the morning when we commend the new day and the work before us to God.

They open up vast horizons as we pray for:

- the universal Church and all its members: pastors, brothers and sisters, couples, young people, the sick and the persecuted, separated Christians;
- the whole world: for those who govern, for the hungry, for prisoners, etc.; for peace and justice among individuals and nations. Through the intercessions, we take upon ourselves "the cries of the poor and the needy."

Just like Mary of the Incarnation in her *Apostolic Prayer*, "we travel around the world to find all the souls" and present them to God the Father. But sadly, our prayers will never meet all the needs of humanity.

After the general intercessions come the spontaneous requests. That's when we pray for our special intentions.

The response is an important element of these prayers, in particular when it is sung. The repeated words tend to etch an idea or feeling in the soul.

The praise and the intercessions follow the rhythm of the week and emphasize:

- Christ's Resurrection on Sundays;
- the mystery of the Cross on Fridays;
- the memory of Our Lady on Saturdays.

Sometimes, the intercessions are taken from ancient litanies—litanies of the Saints, the prayers of Pope Clement, of Saint Gelasius—or from the Byzantine liturgy. Fortunately, in the latter case, the translation has kept the original response *Kyrie eleison* in order to underline our union with the Eastern Churches.

The *Didachè* or *Doctrine of the Twelve Apostles*, a book that goes back to the origins of Christianity (around A.D. 150), invited the faithful to recite the Lord's Prayer three times a day, morning, noon, and evening. It was taught by Jesus Himself to His disciples and it synthesizes all prayers. It puts us before God as His children and teaches us that we are brothers and sisters, since we say "Our Father" and we ask for "our" daily bread. Today, the Church still recites what has become the Sunday prayer at the celebration of the Eucharist and in the morning and evening Hours. It can be introduced by a short admonition, which allows the congregation to stress the two most important words: "Our Father."

At the close of each Hour, it is up to the presider to recite the collect. As representative of Christ, Head of the Church, he "collects" the congregation's intentions, hence the name of this prayer. Though brief, it is very rich and beautiful and it reminds us of the feast being celebrated or the meaning of the Hour. The collect helps us to pray together with the universal Church and often connects us with the Eucharist.

After the blessing given by the celebrant, the congregation disperses.

Is there any father among you who would hand his son a snake when he asks for a fish, or hand him a scorpion when he asks for an egg? If you, then, despite your evil nature, know how to give good things to your children, how much more will the heavenly Father give the Holy Spirit to those who ask Him!   (Lk 11:11-13)

15

THE LITURGY OF THE HOURS
AND SPIRITUALITY

The *Liturgy of the Hours* is a means of developing spirituality.

We cannot recite psalms every day, listen to the Word, sing God's praises without discovering the greatness of the Lord Jesus, His paschal mystery, and the mercy of God. How could we celebrate the Divine Office for years without becoming part of the history of salvation and the Mystical Body, without feeling that we are on the road to the Heavenly Jerusalem in communion with all the Saints?

True, the celebration of the Hours presupposes a careful preparation. To this end, we must know the Bible, study the psalms, learn about the liturgy.

The renewal of the liturgy will not bear all its fruit without adequate theology and catechesis. There are no short cuts. Celebrating the Hours implies a profound capacity for prayer. That is a gift from God, since it is the Spirit Who prays through us "with sighs that cannot be put into words" (Rom 8:26) and Who teaches us to say: "*Abba*, Father" or "Jesus is Lord."

However, contemplative prayer can only be mastered after a long period of training. It requires a pure heart, free of evil passions, capable of silence and attention to God, open to the Spirit.

In that sense, we can say that prayer fits into life and life fits into prayer. Cardinal Martini, bishop emeritus of Milan, writes this about the celebration of the Eucharist: "In order to understand and receive the riches of this mystery, we must respect and be intensely involved in the pauses, the moments of silence, of personal worship and communal contemplation, as specified in the celebration ritual. The spirit of worship born out of the celebration tends to spread to other areas outside the celebration." This applies perfectly to the *Liturgy of the Hours*.

The *Liturgy of the Hours* is a powerful moment in a life that is itself a celebration.

According to the Council's instructions, far from eliminating personal prayer, the Office both presupposes and gives rise to it, for it offers an authentic "source of piety and a nourishment for personal prayer" (SC 90).

The Lord Himself shows His disciples the twofold manner in which to pray. He does recommend communal praying in His words related by Matthew in chapter 18, but He also insists that we speak to our Heavenly Father behind closed doors in the secret of our room (Mt 6:6). There are many ways of doing it, but praying in silence is essential to prepare and to prolong the celebration of the liturgy.

When we pray after communion, we often ask to remain in a permanent state of thanksgiving. Just as the Eucharist lives on in our souls, the Office continues through silent prayer, contemplation, worship before the Holy Sacrament, thus turning our very life into a liturgy, "a spiritual sacrifice" in the service of God and mankind.

The *Liturgy of the Hours* demands discipline, a form of asceticism since we must set aside specific times in the morning and in the evening for the Divine service.

In the midst of our hectic lives, full of activities in the outside world, the Office provides an excellent opportunity to collect our thoughts and to show steadfast devotion and obedience to the Holy Spirit. Indeed, the communal prayer of the whole Church is based on very concrete requirements: adhering to a predetermined timetable, respecting the congregation's rhythm, making a permanent effort to improve the quality of the singing and chanting, preparing adequately for the Office.

It is impossible to be of one heart and soul without giving up our individual selves.

We must be receptive to the *Liturgy of the Hours*. It is not the product of our preferences or personal taste, nor of our imagination or ideology, even though it does allow for certain choices.

In the liturgy, it is God Who speaks through the Scriptures, and the Holy Spirit inspires the words of our prayers through the psalms.

When we celebrate the Office, our faith is nourished by the faith of the Church. In it, we find an overview of our beliefs that is both rich and balanced.

The Church presents all aspects of the Christian mystery and opens up the sources of Revelation. If we rely on our own prayers, we may tend to favor the points of view that please us and set aside the ones that don't suit us. A prayer handed down by the Church forces us to go beyond our purely individual concerns and immediate preferences, which are often limited and motivated by self-interest.

To welcome God's Word doesn't mean to choose what we like, but rather to accept everything that it says, everything it communicates through the Church.

This "obedience of faith," as Saint Paul calls it, does not exclude spontaneity; on the contrary, it purifies and educates it.

The daily celebration of the Office requires and at the same time cultivates a sense of praise, putting us before the greatness, beauty and infinite love of God as they are revealed through creation, the history of salvation, and the mystery of Christ.

The texts from the Bible, the psalms in particular, make us "enjoy the beauty of the LORD and gaze on His temple" (Ps 27:4).

His temple is the Universe,
It is Jesus Christ,
It is the soul where His Spirit dwells.

Deep within ourselves, contemplation spreads light, peace, and joy; it prompts us to bless our Creator and Savior in the midst of everything that happens to us. We then join in the symphonic jubilation of the cosmos, the Church, the heavenly liturgy described in the Book of Revelation.

A prayer without joy is offensive to God.
(Max Thurian)

On the Cross, the Savior offers up His prayers and His tears to redeem the world. Prayer plays an essential role in God's plan for salvation. Bishops and priests cannot practice their ministry without constantly praying. They sanctify the people through their intercession united with Christ's. By so doing, they contribute to "bringing growth to God's people in a hidden but fruitful apostolate" (GI 18).

It is an admirable power that has been placed into their hands, but it is also the first duty of those who participate in the priestly duty of the Good Shepherd. We can see once more the primary importance of the liturgy for all those, be they lay or religious, who have received an apostolic calling. Today as in the past, the Divine Office is an instrument of evangelization. Furthermore, the *Liturgy of the Hours* involves the laity in the saving mission of the Church.

The ecclesial community thus exercises a true maternal function in bringing souls to

Christ, not only by charity, good example and works of penance but also by prayer (GI 17).

The Council's Constitution *Sacrosanctum Concilium* has clearly defined the place of our prayers within the Church: "every liturgical celebration . . . is an action of Christ the priest and of His Body which is the Church" (SC 7). The Word incarnate is intimately present inside and among us each time we are gathered in His name. Saint Augustine said time and again: "He prays for us as priest, He prays in us as our head, He is the object of our prayer as our God."

Liturgical prayer is never an individual one; it is communal by nature; it opens our hearts so that we may commune with our brothers and sisters of the Church in a "sacrament of unity" (SC 26), and thus collaborate in "building up the mystical Body of Christ, and for the good of the local churches" (GI 24).

Finally, our earthly liturgy is closely akin to the celestial one. We sing a hymn to the glory of the Lord with the multitude of Angels and Saints in Heaven. We journey towards the homeland where God is everything in everyone; our celebrations give us a foretaste of the liturgy in the Jerusalem up above (SC 8).

In Christ, we are all but one man whose head is in heaven and whose limbs still toil on earth.   (Saint Augustine)

16

A CELEBRATION

The prayer of the Hours is not just a reading, nor a simple recitation; it is truly a joyous, meditative celebration.

Any celebration implies certain postures, gestures and signs; it requires simplicity and a sense of elation because the liturgy is a feast.

Saint Jerome said: "Bringing the faithful together is always a feast." Our bodies have the right and the duty to take part in the celebration. No one can pray only with the spirit.

For that reason, the place of the celebration is not immaterial. We are all aware of the importance of our surroundings and the prevailing atmosphere; they can make it easier or more difficult to lift our hearts up unto the Lord. Beauty and prayer go hand in hand because praying means contemplating the supreme Beauty. Cardinal Martini wrote a pastoral letter on the beauty that saves the world, the "ancient and new beauty" referred to by Saint Augustine.

Generally speaking, the communal celebration of the *Liturgy of the Hours* is best recited in a church or a chapel. We must always choose a fitting place, one well decorated, that favors meditation. The rubrics specify that liturgical vestments are to be worn for the solemn offices (GI 255). It is a fact that vestments and ornaments contribute to creating the right atmosphere. As for statues and icons, they remind us of the mystery being celebrated or of the Saint whose day it is; according to the wishes of Vatican II, they should be truly artistic. Flowers and candles shall adorn the altar, the tabernacle, the cross, the lectern, or the statues.

The color of the vestments evokes the time in the liturgical cycle. The lectern may be covered with a cloth in the day's color for the reading of the Word of God.

During the Easter season, the paschal candle, symbol of the risen Christ, will be lit at least for the most important celebrations.

Light is in itself a significant symbol. The menorah, a seven-branch candelabra, had pride of place in the Temple in Jerusalem. The Book of Revelation describes seven fire torches burning before the heavenly throne (Rev 4:5).

In our own liturgy, candles and lamps remind us of Christ, Light of the world. When we were baptized, we received a light which must remain lit until the end.

Light means celebration, rejoicing, praying with perseverance.

In the Temple of the Old Law, incense was burned on the golden altar day and night as a sacrifice of praise. St. John saw an Angel before God's throne in Heaven, with a golden censer in his hand: "The smoke of the incense together with the prayers of the Saints rose before God from the hand of the Angel" (Rev 8:4).

The custom of burning incense comes from that, especially during the Canticles of Mary and Zechariah, at morning and evening prayer.

> To accept joyfully that the church and the celebrations be beautiful is to accept the requirements and the laws of Incarnation.
>
> (Max Thurian)

The postures and external signs express the unity of the congregation through its active participation in the liturgy. The first sign is the community itself: by its external behavior, it shows its communal and hierarchical, and its pilgrim and joyous character.

The arrangement of people is especially important. A group of persons scattered about the church does not convey a sense of unity, quite the contrary.

Among the gestures that accompany the *Liturgy of the Hours*, those that are rooted in a long Christian tradition should be renewed. Gestures help us to stand before God and teach us to adopt the appropriate attitude in His presence. We don't pray with words alone; there is a body language that suits the feelings expressed, a symbolism in gestures that conveys humility, repentance, respect, joy, and adoration. We can see the characters in the Bible and Jesus Himself praying on their knees, bowing low, standing, with hands raised.

The Sign of the Cross is a profession of faith in the mystery of the Holy Trinity and Redemption. It also serves as a reminder of our Baptism through which we joined a priestly people, a holy nation called to take part in the Church's prayer.

We make the Sign of the Cross:

- at the beginning of each hour;
- at the start of the Gospel Canticles;
- at the final blessing.

Standing while praying signals availability, respect, vigilance. It symbolizes the pilgrim's readiness to start on his way, the servant's attention to his master's commands. This attitude stems from the Judeo-Christian tradition.

He who listens and meditates, stops and sits down. This is the attitude of the wise, contemplative man. The Gospel tells us that "Mary . . . sat at the Lord's feet and listened to what He was saying" (Lk 10:39).

The early Christians prayed with their hands raised and outstretched. This gesture implies openness to God, to our brothers and sisters, and is particularly suited to the *Our Father*.

Monks still bow to express humility, respect, and repentance.

Why not invent other exterior expressions of feelings that better correspond to the attitudes of new generations and the requirements of different cultures?

The catechists will make sure that the new gestures and signs are properly explained. It will also remind everyone that communal prayer demands asceticism not only of the spirit but also of the body.

As Saint Cyprian tells us: "The eye of God must delight in the bearing of the body and the sound of the voice."

The presider plays an important role in creating a climate of meditation every time that he listens carefully to the Word, recites a passage, prays silently or out loud. His gestures and the tone of his voice should be an inspiration for the assembled faithful. It has been said: "An absent-minded presider distracts the congregation's attention." The reverse is also true: "A presider who prays fervently helps the entire community to pray."

The various ministers must be chosen according to their aptitudes. To celebrate any part of the Office is neither a reward nor a privilege; it is a service. Not everyone is a gifted reader or singer, nor does everyone know how to inspire a congregation. Saint Paul tells us that the Spirit distributes the gifts in such a way as to demonstrate the many facets of a single, united Church. So let the different charisms be acknowledged and developed; the beauty of the celebration can only be enhanced.

The Council speaks of the "sacred silence." The Office that emerged from Vatican II contains fewer psalms. This reform aimed at a quieter, more peaceful celebration. It is recommended to intersperse it with silent pauses so as to let the Spirit's voice echo in our hearts and unite more closely our personal prayer to the Word of God.

A moment of silence after each psalm or after the biblical reading helps us to savor the text and contemplate the Lord's wonders.

At the beginning of each Hour, a moment of silent reflection prepares our souls to pray.

The liturgical norms stress the intimate connection between the Divine Office and the celebration of the Eucharist which "finds an excellent preparation in the *Liturgy of the Hours*" and continues through it at different moments of the day (GI 12). Madeleine Delbrel writes: "Liturgical prayer is inseparable from the sacraments; it is entirely centered on the Eucharist and on the Mystery of the Lord's Last Supper."

On Sundays and feast days, as on special times of the liturgical cycle (Advent, Lent, the Paschal season), the collect at the end underlines precisely this unity between the Eucharist and the Divine Office. In the collect, we ask three times—in the morning, in the evening, and at the celebration of the Eucharist—the special grace for the day. For this reason, the choice of Office normally corresponds to that of the Eucharist. It is suggested that we meditate on these prayers which are often beautiful compositions.

The practices in use leave enough room for creativity, for instance in the spontaneous intentions, the homily, even the choice of Office, to take into account the type of congregation or personal devotion. True creativity is always respectful of the faith and the laws of the Church and is inspired by intelligent flexibility. It makes praying easier and more authentic.

In conclusion, we can say that the liturgy is flexible in its rules and full of riches: it gives us the possibility to build up the Church and glorify the Lord. Without a doubt, it requires effort and dialogue on the part of the community. It is easy to fall into improvisation or a monotonous routine. What John Paul II says about the Eucharist equally applies to the the Hours: *It is appropriate and absolutely essential to develop an intensive education to bring forth the riches contained in the present liturgy.*

An authentic celebration of the Hours cannot be improvised nor invented: it must be prepared. And so we should explore all the avenues opened up by the post-reform liturgy.

The overriding consideration is to ensure that the celebration is not too inflexible or over-elaborate or concerned only with merely formal observance but matches the reality of what is celebrated. One must strive above all to inspire hearts with a desire for genuine prayer and to show that the celebration of God's praise is a thing of joy (see Psalm 147). (GI 279)

Before changing anything, it is very important to study carefully the suggested texts to make sure that nothing essential is rejected. Received and promulgated by the Church, these texts play a vital role in the making of a Christian.   (Joseph Gélineau)

APPENDIX

Different Voices*

As we read the various psalms in the Hours, we are often filled with amazement at how they may exactly express what we ourselves are feeling. If our hearts are singing with joy, the psalms of Morning Prayer may echo our gratitude to God and our praise for his goodness. If our hearts and minds are burdened with sorrow and distress, the psalms of the Office of Readings or Evening Prayer may echo our grief. If people in our lives harass or harm us, how well we find ourselves able to cry out to heaven in the words of the psalmist!

Ambrose well describes the wonderful nature of the psalms as sources of prayer for people in many different states:[11]

> In the Book of Psalms there is profit for all, with healing power for our salvation. There is instruction from history, teaching from the law, prediction from prophecy, chastisement from denunciation, persuasion from moral preaching. All who read it may find the cure for their own individual failings. All with eyes to see can dis-

---

* "Different Voices" is taken from *A Companion to the Liturgy of the Hours* by Shirley Darcus Sullivan, © 2004, Catholic Book Publishing Corp., pp. 14-17.

[11] *Explanation of the Psalms*, Ps. 1:4, in *Office of Readings* in *The Liturgy of the Hours* (as in note 12), Vol. 3, p. 343.

cover in it a complete gymnasium for the soul, a stadium for all the virtues, equipped for every kind of exercise; it is for *all* to choose the kind they *judge* best to help *them* gain the prize.

First and foremost, therefore, the psalms can be our own voice, praying with earnest devotion to God. We become one with the psalmist as the words express the thoughts and feelings of our souls. This possible identification helps to make the reading of the psalms meaningful. On a deeper level, it makes praying the psalms a personal encounter with God. Our feelings and circumstances are immediately present in the words we say.

The *Liturgy of the Hours*, however, is always much more than our own personal prayer. It is the prayer of the whole Church, uttered in many, many languages around the world. Thus, Ambrose says of the psalms:[12]

> Yes, a psalm is a blessing on the lips of the people, a hymn in praise of God, the assembly's homage, a general acclamation, a word that speaks for all, the voice of the Church, a confession of faith in song. It is the voice of complete assent, the joy of freedom, a cry of happiness, the echo of gladness.

Praying the psalms involves a "liturgy," a sacred act inspired by the Holy Spirit.[13] Thus, in a sense, one voice ascends to God from his

---

[12] *Explanation of the Psalms*, Ps. 1:9 (as in note 12), Vol. 3, p. 347.
[13] On this meaning of "liturgy" see H. M. Roguet, OP, *The Liturgy of the Hours*, trans. P. Coughlan and P. Purdue, Collegeville, MN: Liturgical Press, 1971, pp. 84-88.

Church. This is the voice of all the baptized rendering praise to God as is his due.

Yet, on a deeper level, there is another presence to be found in the psalms. The psalms proclaim the life and mission of Jesus. Once again Ambrose speaks clearly of this aspect of the psalms:[14]

> What am I to say of the grace of prophecy? We see that what others hinted at in riddles was promised openly and clearly to the psalmist alone: the Lord Jesus was to be born of David's seed, according to the word of the Lord, *I will place upon your throne one who is the fruit of your flesh.*
>
> In the psalms, then, not only is Jesus born for us, he also undergoes his saving passion in his body, he lies in death, he rises again, he ascends into heaven, he sits at the right hand of the Father. What no one would have dared to say was foretold by the psalmist alone, and afterward proclaimed by the Lord himself in the Gospel.

Yet in the psalms we can go a step deeper. We must not only learn about Jesus but also hear his voice in prayer. But which Jesus is this? Jesus, we know, is now reigning in heaven in the presence of his Father, the angels, and all the saints. Which Jesus would be praying in the psalms? This Jesus is he who is present in the souls of all the faithful, in your soul and my soul.

---

[14] *Explanation of the Psalms,* Ps. 1:7-8 (as in note 12), Vol. 3, p. 344.

This voice of Jesus is present in the Hours; it is a voice that prays to the Father.[15] Always the Church identifies with Jesus as he obeys the Father and offers him praise. In the Hours this activity of Jesus appears to be particularly evident. If we remember that it is Jesus, present within our souls, who is praying, we can partake in the Hours in a profoundly spiritual way. This perspective helps us to move beyond ourselves into a new level of consciousness.

What happens if we listen for the voice of Jesus? Psalms take on a new richness and depth not perceived before. We are constantly drawn out of our own limited experience into a deeper way of praying. For example, on some occasions, we may encounter a psalm full of sorrow although we, at that moment, are not experiencing grief. If we listen for the voice of Jesus, we can forget ourselves and try to see things from his point of view. So too with psalms expressing joy, wonder, delight, we can see the experiences they describe as those of Jesus. When the psalmist cries out in pain or in anguish over the treatment received from enemies, we can move out of our own lives and ponder deeply the sufferings of Jesus. As Christians, we are called to love Jesus and, by loving him, to be transformed into him:

Although you have not seen him, you love him; and even though you do not see him now yet

---

[15] Roguet, pp. 87-88.

believe in him, you rejoice with an indescribable and glorious joy, as you attain the goal of [your] faith, the salvation of your souls (1 Peter 1:8).

He has bestowed on us the precious and very great promises, so that through them you may come to share in the divine nature (2 Peter 1:4).

The more we hear the voice of Jesus in the psalms, the more we will come to understand who he is and what we are called to be.

In terms of voices, therefore, the Hours may be our own voice, the voice of the Church, or the voice of Jesus. The possibility of these different voices allows us to enter in an individual yet universal way into the Hours. It also, in particular, allows us to share in the prayer that Jesus makes to the Father. We take part in the "liturgy," the holy act by which God is praised.[16] The psalms reveal the whole range of human experience in which Jesus shared. The Hours make this sharing present now in our time. The voice of Jesus sanctifies all that human beings feel and suffer and offers all to the Father. The more we pray the Hours, the more our voice and the voice of the Church become the voice of Jesus. We enter ever more deeply into the life of prayer. We move from "saying" the Hours ourselves to "praying" the Hours ourselves and then, at a deeper level, to "praying" the Hours with Jesus, in close identity with his Church.

---

[16] Roguet, pp. 87-91.

Reading the Bible Prayerfully and Holistically

The Stages of *Lectio Divina* in Contemporary Terms

Utilizing the Bible's repetitive, affirming, and multiple perspective approach, I will now present the activities and dynamics of *lectio divina* in contemporary terms using alliteration. In the psalms, this technique is known as acrostic. It is designed to be mnemonic, that is, facilitate memorization and retention.

Lectio divina consists of activities that typically unfold in stages, though not necessarily sequentially. Not only does each person process the Bible and life experience uniquely, but such changes with the circumstances and the person's development.

Traditionally, *lectio's* stages have been identified as *reading, meditation, prayer, contemplation,* and *action.* The following alliterative parallels serve as a starting and reference point for the discussion of the traditional stages that follow.

• **Retreat (Refresh/Restore/Renew):** Step back from the hustle-bustle. Make time for daily Sabbath moments.

• **Relax:** Come into God's presence and get settled in, as you would with a friend.

* "Reading the Bible Prayerfully and Holistically" is taken from the *St. Joseph Guide to Lectio Divina* by Karl A. Schultz, © 2010, Catholic Book Publishing Corp., pp. 25-36.

• **Release:** Let God free you of unnecessary anxiety and concerns.

• **Read** . . . slowly, aloud, using all the senses, perhaps following the words with your finger to slow down. This naturally heightens your awareness of the grammatical elements of the text, which also communicate meaning. Select a word, phrase, image, or verse(s) from the passage that touches or teaches you. This "word" can serve as your bridge to the day, a centering point to return to amid the day's activities.

• **Rhythm:** Enter into the flow of God's word and Spirit through gentle oscillation (ranging back and forth) between the various activities. Don't cultivate rigid expectations of what the rhythm should feel like, or worry that you don't have it. It comes naturally with practice and grace, and it is unique to each person.

• **Repeat/Recite:** Gently murmur or recite your "word" repeatedly. This ingrains it in your conscious and subconscious mind as an inspired affirmation.

• **Reflect:** Consider what actions or attitudes your "word" is calling you to. What does it mean to you?

• **Reminisce:** Your "word" may trigger memories of other biblical or life passages. The Hebrew word "*pesach*" from which comes the word "paschal" (i.e., mystery, lamb) refers to the Passover and means passage, which is the essence of Christian life: a journey home. (See *The Art of Passing Over* by Francis Dorff.) *Reminiscence* (the word coined by the medieval monks to describe this practice) helps you connect the various passages, biblical and experiential, in your life. Like reminiscence, passages link things.

• **Re-create:** Use your imagination to envision the biblical scene and character(s). Our objective is to interact with and imaginatively participate in the text holistically, that is, with all our faculties. To use St. Ignatius of Loyola's terminology, "consider the persons" (identify and perhaps dialogue with them).

• **React:** Share your thoughts and feelings with God, others, or your journal.

• **Receive:** Be present to God in silence. Listen. Experience divine consolation.

• **Rest:** Cool down as preparation for resuming your activities. *Lectio divina* is a spiritual exercise that requires both exertion and relaxation.

• **Respond:** Don't just pray; do something. Practice what you have received.

• **Realize:** Enjoy the fruits of your labor. Discover God's initiative in your life. Experience your "word" bearing fruit in your life in various degrees as described in the parable of the sower (cf. Mk 4:2-20).

Lectio Divina's Fluid Nature

Lectio divina is an adaptable, flexible model rather than a rigid method. It isn't a mechanical, linear process. It is fluid, personal, and circumstantial. You oscillate between its stages according to your capacities, circumstances, and the movement of the Spirit. We even change our approach to *lectio* as we grow and our circumstances change. *Lectio* is a dynamic rather than static practice.

Because the activities of *lectio divina* overlap and are related, it is artificial to distinguish between them rigidly. *Lectio divina* is a form of prayer, spiritual communications, and development, and therefore it is not amenable to precise description. Everyone experiences it differently. Like intimacy between spouses, terminology cannot adequately capture the experience.

For example, reading and meditation are essentially two aspects of the same activity of taking in and responding to a biblical or life passage. Prayer and contemplation are the active and receptive aspects of dialogue with God. The early Church originally described this process in terms of reading and prayer. Meditation was considered part of reading, and contemplation was part of prayer. As mentioned, the fifth stage, action, initially was assumed. In the Middle Ages, it was articulated as the consummating stage.

The Vatican II document on Scripture, "The Dogmatic Constitution on Divine Revelation," also known as *Dei Verbum* ("The word of God"), does not specifically mention *lectio divina* by name, though it refers to it through the ancient formula "reading and prayer." Consider how far the Church has come in its promotion of *lectio divina* among the laity. At Vatican II, they didn't even use the term. Now, the pope can hardly give an address or

publish a document on the Bible without mention-
ing *lectio divina*, usually in enthusiastic terms.

Lectio divina continues to evolve with its envi-
ronment: Cardinal Martini of Milan has shown
how the components of discernment, decision, and
consolation, particularly as understood within the
Jesuit tradition, are operative in *lectio divina*. I
highly recommend his books, which are insightful
and stimulating expositions of key biblical texts
using the model of *lectio divina*.

A fascinating aspect of Martini's ministry is that
prior to becoming archbishop of Milan he was a
renowned professor, "text critic" (expert in ancient
biblical manuscripts), and administrator (rector of
both the Pontifical Biblical Institute and Gregorian
University). This brilliant, cultured academic was
to become the worldwide leader in the renaissance
of *lectio divina* at the grassroots level, and to publish over forty books in multiple languages aimed
primarily at non-academics. Most of his academic
writings are of a highly technical nature. Very few
persons can integrate and communicate academic
and popular understandings in so comprehensive
and compelling a manner.

Publisher and topic permitting, I make it a practice to include in my books, articles written by
peers whom I consider to be at the top of the profession. I want to expose you to diverse, first-rate
perspectives on *lectio* and illustrate my assertion
that there is no one right way to practice it. Take
the various perspectives presented and cull from
each one what works for you, and be patient with

yourself and God while you go through the trial and error process. If something feels natural and comfortable, you should trust it, at least until you discover a better way. Instant results are neither guaranteed nor necessary. God calls us to be faithful, rather than successful.

How Does *Lectio* Unfold?

There are as many permutations of *lectio* as there are persons and settings. What you do today may be different from tomorrow. For example, you might begin by reading and then be led by the Spirit to the silence of contemplation. Or perhaps you'll begin by praying your feelings and then move to meditation on your current situation in light of the biblical passage you are reading or reminded of (reminiscence). You might also begin and linger in the silence of contemplation, soaking up God's presence. When you're weary, just being with a loved one is what you need most.

The key is to follow where your faculties and the prompting of the Spirit take you, while eventually incorporating each of the stages. You thereby balance spontaneity and self-discipline, and avoid being too rigid or scrupulous or too lax. Catholicism is a religion of balance, integration, and moderation, attributes that characterize the Bible and human development as well.

Lectio Lesson

Without being scrupulous or mechanical, it is important to incorporate some degree of each of the *lectio* activities at some point in a given session. (This usually happens naturally, so we need not be hyper-conscious of it.) Otherwise our experience may be unbalanced, and even counterproductive, for example:

• If we don't pray, we don't share ourselves with God.

• If we don't engage in contemplation, and thereby listen and rest in God's presence, we won't open ourselves fully to His guidance.

• If we don't read, we lose touch with the inspired source material and fundamental activity, reading. We are unable to inform our prayer with the "word" from the text. Of course, prayer can exist independent of reading, but the advantage of reading is that it gives us divinely inspired substance for our reflections.

• If we don't meditate, the word we received in the reading stage won't take root in us.

• If we don't act on the word, it is lifeless.

An influential medieval proponent of *lectio*, the twelfth century Carthusian monk Guigo II, offers the following helpful synthesis:

" . . . reading without meditation is sterile, meditation without reading is liable to error, prayer without meditation is lukewarm, meditation without prayer is unfruitful, prayer when it is fervent wins contemplation, but to obtain it without prayer would be rare, even miraculous. However, there is no limit to God's power, and His merciful love surpasses all His other works" (Guigo II, *The Ladder of Monks*).

The Holistic Nature of *Lectio Divina*

Different faculties come to the forefront in each stage of *lectio divina.* Just as it is artificial to distinguish precisely between the stages of *lectio divina,* so the various faculties engaged [sensate (reading), mental (meditation), unconscious mind (meditation), affective/emotions (prayer), spiritual (prayer, contemplation), and in a group, social/relational] are likewise intertwined and not readily divisible. This integration yields a positive by-product: usage of all our faculties during *lectio* translates to spontaneous incorporation in daily life. *Lectio*, like Catholic and biblical spirituality in general, is not compartmentalized. The habits and attitudes we cultivate naturally spill over to the rest of our life.

This holistic or integrated characteristic also applies on the moral level: the way we practice love of God, self, and neighbor with our whole heart, mind, and strength (cf. Mk 12:28-34), and how it forms us as whole persons according to Jesus' commands (cf. Mt 5:48).

Retreat

I use the term "retreat" as both a noun and a verb. It is a description of the purpose and mentality underlying *lectio* as well as an informal stage or activity. A retreat is a traditional spiritual practice of getting away (retreating) for a day, a weekend, or more to reflect on God's word and discern His activity in your life. You can call it an expanded Sabbath or a spiritual vacation.

Lectio is meant to be a periodic Sabbath moment bridged to our activities and daily life through application of the "word" we have received. It is a retreat from our hustle-bustle existence for purposes of slowing down, taking stock of life, and discerning God's will and initiative. Even a few minutes can be a regenerating oasis of calm. View *lectio* as a retreat rather than a burden. It is time to be refreshed and renewed by God's word.

Relaxing

Traditionally, relaxing has not been articulated as a stage of *lectio divina*. However, given the hectic nature of modern life and cultural pressures working against the *shalom* (peace/wholeness) that God offers us, it seems prudent to articulate relaxing as a preparatory stage.

As with a couple who have been away from each other for awhile, we need time to get used to a more immediate experience of God's presence, and temporarily let go of anxieties and distractions. Otherwise we will not be able to tune in to God's subtle *modus operandi*, the still, small voice (cf. 2 Kings 19:12).

To use a eucharistic image, when you share a special meal with someone, you usually don't jump right in to an intense discussion. (At Mass we build up to the consecration.) You get an initial reading on yourself, your counterpart, and the situation, and then enter into a mode of interaction conducive to a deeper engagement of mind and heart.

Our ancestors knew how to relax and slow down. They didn't live in a secular, materialistic, productivity-oriented culture like ours. They didn't need to articulate relaxation as a stage because they did it naturally. We need to remind ourselves and take steps to facilitate relaxation. Examples of such include deep breathing, guided imagery, and awareness exercises. Physical exercise is also helpful for getting emotional toxins out of our system and clearing our mind.

Relaxation is neither an escape nor a shirking of responsibilities. It is a spiritual form of leisure that is not akin to "wasting time." By giving ourselves time to relax and become conscious of God's welcome and presence, we're more disposed to hear His word and receive His graces.

Reading/Listening/Sensing (*Lectio*)

Lectio divina is unlike most styles of reading you have experienced. You read slowly and rhythmically, almost the antithesis of speed-reading. You'll eventually settle into a rhythm and pace that facilitates internalization of God's word.

If feasible, read aloud or in an almost imperceptible whisper or undertone. Sometimes your energy level or the circumstances dictate that you read silently, but if at all possible try speaking or whispering the word. Ancient physicians prescribed reading as a form of exercise. When you try reading aloud, you'll know why. It requires effort and energy!

When you read aloud, you use all of your senses. Yes, even taste and smell. The medieval monks who practiced *lectio divina* spoke of tasting the word by savoring its sweetness and mouthing or speaking the words in a careful, reverential way.

Can you smell God's word? Literally no, but metaphorically yes. Beginning with St. Paul, spiritual writers have spoken of spirituality in terms of an aroma (cf. 2 Cor 2:15). Using our imagination, we can sense the terrain on which Jesus traversed, the fragrance of the flowers he admired, and the smell of farm animals, laborers, travelers, and fishermen.

This engagement of the senses is one reason I emphasized relaxing as a necessary preparation. The more relaxed and present you are, the less impaired your senses will be, and the more readily you will engage them.

As a holistic side effect, using all of your senses engages your imagination, and this naturally translates to the way you experience life, i.e., more sensately and holistically. With greater familiarity with *lectio divina* and the Bible, you will have a fuller experience of the sensate dimensions of the text and life.

Spiritual Grazing: Nibbling on the Word

In practicing *lectio divina*, we're not concerned with covering a preordained amount of the Bible in one sitting. Just as an unexpected event or brief interpersonal encounter can have significant repercussions and evoke intense reactions and reflection, so a small portion of the Bible can go a long way.

We typically begin with a small passage of Scripture. Precisely how much is not important.

We read until some word, verse, image, theme, or perhaps a related personal experience or biblical text strikes us. We then take in and reflect on that stimulus. See the *St. Joseph Guide to the Bible* for recommended reading plans with respect to the Bible.

Good things come in small passages. One of the side effects of sampling a small portion of Scripture is the humility and calm it instills. It slows us down. We lose any pretense of being a master of the word or the world. In the spirit of Psalm 131, we don't set our eyes on the heights of personal gratification. Rather, we satisfy ourselves to be nurtured by the Lord. A small portion of Scripture, taken to heart, is more than enough to nourish and challenge us.

I use the term spiritual grazing quite literally, as the back and forth movement of the ruminant animal recalls the ancient pastoral image associated with *lectio divina* as well as the traditional Jewish practice of *shukkling*, that is, rocking back and forth in response to the energy generated by a holistic encounter with God's word. Perhaps the most familiar example of this is at the Wailing Wall in Jerusalem.

In giving our whole selves to a small portion of Scripture, we buck the consumption mentality of our times. Instead of mechanically devouring God's word and hurriedly going on to the next activity or stimulus, we savor it and let it permeate our being and influence our attitudes and actions.

What if no word stands out and we feel unmoved by the biblical passage? Don't worry about it. Accept what comes, even if it's only the slightest of inspirations or consolations (e.g., peaceful sensations; cf. Phil 4:7). *Lectio divina* isn't a results-oriented competition in which we are judged by how much Scripture speaks to us. God will provide what we need. Our job is to make time for God, offer ourselves as we are, avoid sloppiness, presumption, and lethargy, and keep at it (cf. Mt 24:46; Lk 8:15; 21:19): "Rejoice in hope, endure in affliction, persevere in prayer" (Rom 12:12).

Meditation (*Meditatio*)

Once we have identified a portion of Scripture that speaks to us, our next step is to experience that text in all its richness. Savor and internalize it through repetitive recitation or murmuring. Pope Benedict describes it this way:

"Among the many fruits of this biblical spring-time I would like to mention the spread of the ancient practice of *lectio divina* or 'spiritual reading' of Sacred Scripture. It consists in pouring over a biblical text for some time, reading it and rereading it, as it were, 'ruminating' on it as the Fathers say and squeezing from it, so to speak, all its 'juice,' so that it may nourish meditation and contemplation and, like water, succeed in irrigating life itself," (Benedict XVI, November 6, 2005).

In biblical and patristic times, the most frequent image associated with meditation was of a cow or goat *ruminating* (chewing its cud). Psalm

1:2 advocates murmuring or reciting God's word repeatedly.

Utilizing Our Memories

Our memories are not as active or as developed as our ancestors'. Without the benefit of communication storage media, they had more need and practice. Most people today can remember only a small portion of Scripture. Repetitively reciting Scripture enlarges our capacity for God's word, just as it did our ancestors'. Murmuring or whispering the words repetitively can ingrain them in our memory. Not only do we remember it better, but we internalize and assimilate it, making it a part of us.

One byproduct of becoming a consistent practitioner of *lectio divina* is that of increased awareness of the potentialities of our faculties, many of which are often underutilized (e.g., our memories, and subconscious mind), and of God and the Church's desire that we develop ourselves to the fullest. *Lectio divina* engages our whole self in surrender to the divine will and for the good of ourselves, the Church, and the world. Accordingly, it helps us fulfill our individual and communal potential.

In his March 26, 1967 encyclical *Populorum Progressio* ("On the Development of Peoples"), Pope Paul VI observed:

"In the design of God, every man is called upon to develop and fulfill himself, for every life is a vocation.

"By the unaided effort of his own intelligence and his will, each man can grow in humanity, can enhance his personal worth, can become more a person. However, this self-fulfillment is not something optional. Just as the whole of creation is ordained to its Creator, so spiritual beings should of their own accord orientate their lives to God, the first truth and the supreme good. Thus it is that human fulfillment constitutes, as it were, a summary of our duties.

". . . But there is much more: this harmonious enrichment of nature by personal and responsible effort is ordered to a further perfection. By reason of his union with Christ, the source of life, man attains to new fulfillment of himself, to a transcendent humanism which gives him his greatest possible perfection: this is the highest goal of personal development."

In his will, Paul VI offered this poignant reflection:

"Why have I not studied, explored, admired sufficiently this place in which life unfolds? What unpardonable distraction, what reprehensible superficiality!"

Beginning with his first encyclical *Redemptor Hominis* ("Redeemer of Man"), and continuing throughout his pontificate, Pope John Paul II focused on the moral, spiritual, and developmental ramifications of human dignity, which was to become his signature theme. His theology of the body teachings (weekly addresses conducted from September, 1979 through November, 1984) were a profound theological anthropology of human development and fulfillment as it relates to human sexuality. The documents of Vatican II, particularly *Gaudium et Spes* ("The Pastoral Constitution on the Church in the Modern World"), and subsequent magisterial teaching likewise emphasized human fulfillment, wellness, and spirituality in all its dimensions, with the recent focus on *lectio divina* being a logical development of this theme. The holistic and dialogical nature of *lectio divina* helps us fulfill the first and second commandments (cf. Mt 22:34-40), which mandate the gift of our whole and true selves to God and neighbor.

GLOSSARY

Advent. Church year begins with the first Sunday of Advent. The Advent season contains the four Sundays of Advent and the days between them and Christmas.

Alleluia. Biblical cry of joy. Not prayed during Lent.

Alleluia Side. Original name of *Side Two* when praying the Office in choir.

Alternative Prayer. Another concluding prayer to certain offices which may be chosen as an option.

Antiphon. Short, repeated prayer that introduces and follows a Psalm or Canticle in the Divine Office.

Antiphon in Honor of the Blessed Virgin. Prayer following the conclusion of Night Prayer, honoring Mary, the Mother of God.

Antiphon, Easter. Three Alleluias, prayed consecutively.

Antiphonarian. The person who prays the Antiphon and the first line of each Psalm when praying in choir. If two cantors are used, the second is called the Antiphonarian.

Baptism of the Lord. Last day of celebration for the Christmas season. Takes the place of the first Sunday of Ordinary Time.

Benedictus. Traditional name for the Canticle of Zechariah.

breviary. Prayer book that contains the Divine Office.

breviary, four-volume. Contains every prayer of the Divine Office in four volumes.

breviary, one-volume. A single volume that contains complete Morning, Evening, and Night Prayer from the Divine Office and selections from other offices. Also called *Christian Prayer*.

breviary, travelers. A single, thin volume that contains an abbreviated form of the Divine Office. Also called *Shorter Christian Prayer*.

Canticle. Poetic prayer, meant to be sung, found in the Bible.

Canticle of Daniel. Daniel 3:57-88, 56 in the Bible. The only Canticle in the Divine Office after which the Glory Be is not prayed.

Canticle of Mary. Mary's *Magnificat*, sung upon visiting her cousin Elizabeth shortly after Mary conceived Our Lord (Luke 1:46-55), prayed during Evening Prayer.

Canticle of Simeon. Simeon's song of praise upon seeing the Infant Christ in the Temple (Luke 2:29-32), prayed during Night Prayer.

Canticle of Zechariah. Zechariah's song of praise upon the birth of John the Baptist (Luke 1:67-79) prayed during Morning Prayer.

Cantor. Person who sings the Antiphons and leads the singing in the Divine Office. Also called *Hebdomedarian* or *First Cantor*.

chant. Song in which a single note or simple combination of notes is used exclusively.

choir. Praying in choir means praying the Office as a group but alternating sides in the recitation.

Chorus Side. Original name for *Side One* when praying the Office in choir.

Christian Prayer. A common name for the *one-volume breviary*.

Christmas Season. Begins with Christmas Eve and ends with the Baptism of the Lord.

clergy, ordained. All priests and deacons of the Roman Catholic Church.

Commemoration. All Memorials that are celebrated during Lent, during Advent between December 17 to the 23rd, and during the Octave of Christmas become Commemorations. These are optional celebrations.

Common, Primary Office. First Common referred to in any particular celebration.

Common, Secondary Office. Second Common referred to in any particular celebration.

Commons. Offices that can be used for a number of celebrations.

Complementary Psalmody. Part of the Divine Office that contains the Gradual Psalms used in praying the Midmorning, Midday, and Midafternoon Offices.

Compline. Traditional name for *Night Prayer*.

Concluding Prayer. Prayer that ends the Divine Office.

Daytime Prayer. When only one office is prayed between Morning and Evening Prayer, that office is called Daytime Prayer.

Divine Office. The official, formal prayer composed by the Church to pray throughout the day.

Easter Season. Begins with the Easter Triduum and ends with Evening Prayer II on Pentecost.

Evening Prayer. Office prayed in the evening.

Evening Prayer Canticle. Another name for the *Canticle of Mary*.

Evening Prayer I. Evening Prayer Office prayed on the eve preceding a Solemnity.

Evening Prayer II. Evening Prayer Office prayed on the eve of a Solemnity.

Examination of Conscience. Made silently at the beginning of Night Prayer as a review of one's actions, words, and thoughts during the day.

Feast. A high celebration of the Church, slightly less important than a Solemnity. A Feast is celebrated by the whole Church.

Ferial Day. Weekdays on which no specific saint is commemorated.

First Reading. Scripture reading in the Office of Readings.

Glory Be. Prayed at the end of every Psalm and Canticle in the Divine Office with the exception of the Canticle of Daniel (Daniel 3:57-88, 56).

Gospel Canticle. Another name for the *Canticle of Simeon*.

Gradual Psalms. Psalms 120-128 used in the Complementary Psalmody.

Guide for Christian Prayer. Another name for an *Ordo*.

Hebdomedarian. Older name for *cantor*.

Hour. Time of prayer.

Hymn. Introduces an office. Traditionally sung but may also be chanted or recited.

Intercessions. Prayers of petition, prayed during Morning and Evening Prayer.

Invitatory. Prayer that invites one to praise God. Begins the first office of the day (either Morning Prayer or the Office of Readings).

Invitatory Psalm. Generally Psalm 95. May also be Psalms 24, 67, or 100.

Lauds. Traditional name for *Morning Prayer*.

Lent. Penitential season in the Church beginning with Ash Wednesday and ending with the start of the Easter Triduum. Forty days in length.

Little Hours. Nickname for the offices of *Midmorning*, *Midday*, and *Midafternoon Prayer*.

Little Offices. Nickname for the offices of *Midmorning, Midday,* and *Midafternoon Prayer.*

Liturgy. Formal rite of the Catholic Church, meant for public worship.

Liturgy of the Hours. Any formal prayers of the Catholic Church that are prayed at certain hours throughout a twenty-four hour day.

Magnificat. Sung by the Mother of Jesus shortly after she conceived Our Lord, recorded in Luke 1:46-55. Prayed during Evening Prayer.

Matins. Traditional Name for the *Office of Readings.*

Memorial. A celebration of the Church that is of less importance than a Feast.

Memorial, Obligatory. A Memorial that must be celebrated by the entire Church.

Memorial, Optional. A Memorial that may be celebrated.

Midafternoon Prayer. Short office prayed about 3 p.m.

Midday Prayer. Short office prayed about noon.

Midmorning Prayer. Short office prayed about 9 a.m.

Morning Prayer. Office prayed in the morning.

Morning Prayer Canticle. Another name for the *Canticle of Zechariah.*

New Testament Canticle. Another name for the *Canticle of Mary.*

Night Prayer. Office prayed right before going to bed.

Night Prayer Canticle. Another name for the *Canticle of Simeon.*

None. Traditional name for *Midafternoon Prayer.*

Nunc Dimittis. Traditional name for the *Canticle of Simeon.*

Octave. Eight days immediately following the Solemnities of Christmas and Easter. The Octave is also celebrated as a Solemnity.

Octave of Christmas. Eight days from Christmas (December 25) through Evening Prayer on the Solemnity of Mary, the Mother of God (January 1).

Octave of Easter. Eight days from Easter Sunday through Evening Prayer on Divine Mercy Sunday (the second Sunday of Easter).

Office. Capitalized, this word refers to the entire Divine Office, which is a series of formal prayers meant to pray throughout the day. With a lower case letter, it refers to a particular part of the entire Office.

Office for the Dead. Office prayed on All Soul's Day. Must be prayed exactly as written in breviary with no substitutions.

Office of Readings. Office that may be prayed any time during the day, consisting of a Psalmody and two long readings.

Old Testament Canticle. Another name for the *Canticle of Zechariah.*

Order, First. Refers to a community of priests and religious brothers who follow the Rule given by their founder.

Order, Religious. Any group of consecrated men or women who follow a Rule of Life common to them all.

Order, Second. Refers to a community of nuns who follow the Rule given by their founder.

Order, Third. Refers to laity who follow a Rule given by a founder of a religious Order.

Ordinary. Section of the breviary that contains general instructions for praying the Divine Office as well as some repeated prayers in the Office.

Ordinary Time. Season of the year that is not Lent/Easter or Advent/Christmas. Consists of thirty-four weeks.

Ordo. A daily guide to praying the Divine Office for an entire year.

Our Father. Prayed in full following the Intercessions in Morning and Evening Prayer.

Poetry Section. Part of the four-volume breviary, used for optional reading. Not part of the Divine Office.

Prayer Leader. When praying in choir, the Prayer Leader reads the first line of Intercessions and the Concluding Prayer.

Prayer of Forgiveness. Prayer after the Examination of Conscience in Night Prayer, asking God's forgiveness of that day's sins.

Presider. A person of rank who opens the office with the Introductory Verse, leads the Intercessions, begins the Lord's Prayer, and prays the Concluding Prayer.

Prime. Office traditionally prayed about the same time as Lauds. Has been suppressed.

Proper of Saints. Contains the entire Office or portions of the Office for all the saints celebrated during the Church year. Each saint has his or her own office for one day of the year.

Proper of Seasons. The section of the Psalter that contains various parts of offices that change with the week and season of the year.

Psalm. A prayer in the Bible, composed to be sung or chanted.

Psalm Prayer. Prayerful reflections that sometimes follow a Psalm or Canticle in the Divine Office.

Psalmody. Part of each office that begins each office and that contains the Psalms for that office.

Psalter. Four-week repeating cycle of Psalms in the Divine Office.

Reader. When praying in choir, the Reader reads the Reading alone and the odd lines of the Responsory (lines 1, 3, 5).

Refrain. A prayer sometimes repeated following each Intercession in the Divine Office.

Response. Abbreviated R in some copies of the Divine Office. Marks part of the Office prayed by all present.

Responsory. Short verses that follow the Reading in the Divine Office.

Rule of Life. Specific ways to live the Christian life, given to a group by a founder.

Season. Three seasons in the Church year: Advent/Christmas; Lent/Easter; Ordinary Time.

Second Reading. Non-scriptural reading in the Office of Readings.

Sext. Traditional name for *Midday Prayer*.

Shorter Christian Prayer. Thin volume of some prayers of the Divine Office.

Side One. When praying in choir, the grouping of individuals who pray the odd strophes of the Psalms (strophes 1, 3, 5, 7, etc.)

Side Two. When praying in choir, the grouping of individuals who pray the even strophes of the Psalms (strophes 2, 4, 6, 8, etc.)

Sign of the Cross. Begins and ends every office and also is made at the beginning of the Canticles of Mary, Zechariah, and Simeon.

Solemnity. A solemn celebration in the Church, the highest Church holiday. It is celebrated by the whole Church. Sunday is always a Solemnity.

Strophe. One section of a Psalm or Canticle, commonly called a *verse*.

Sunday. Always celebrated as a Solemnity.

Sunday Evening Prayer I. Name for the office prayed on Saturday evening.

Sunday Morning Prayer, Week I. The Psalms from this office are used in the observance of Solemnities and Feasts.

Supplement. A book that contains special offices and parts of offices for saints and celebrations particular to a certain Religious Order.

Te Deum. Hymn that is prayed in the Office of Readings after the Second Reading and Responsory on Sundays, Feasts, and Solemnities and during the Octaves of Christmas and Easter. Omitted during Lent.

Terce. Traditional name for *Midmorning Prayer*.

Travelers' Breviary. Thin volume of some prayers of the Divine Office, intended to be lightweight for traveling purposes. Properly called *Shorter Christian Prayer*.

Triduum. Three days of prayer.

Triduum, Easter. Three days of prayer from Holy Thursday Evening Prayer, through Good Friday and Holy Saturday, until Easter. Opens the Easter Season.

Versicle. Abbreviated V in some copies of the Divine Office. Marks part of the Office reserved for the Prayer Leader alone to speak.

Vespers. Traditional name for *Evening Prayer*.

Vigil. The evening immediately preceding a day of celebration.

Vigils. Traditional name for the *Office of Readings*.

Weeks I, II, III, IV. Refer to weeks in the Four Week Psalter in the Divine Office.